# BROODMALES

MANNERS AND CUSTOMS OF THE MIAOTZU
THE COUVADE

From a Chinese manuscript album of the late eighteenth century, the property
of Dr. S. W. Bushell, C.M.G., in the Victoria and Albert Museum, London

*Reproduced by permission of the Director of the Museum*

# BROODMALES

A Psychological Essay on Men
in Childbirth

NOR HALL

Introducing

The Custom of Couvade

WARREN R. DAWSON

Spring Publications, Inc.
Dallas, Texas

"A Psychological Essay on Men in Childbirth" © 1989
by Spring Publications, Inc. All rights reserved
"The Custom of Couvade" first published as a book in 1929
by Manchester University Press, Oxford Road, Manchester
M13 9PL, England. © 1989 by Spring Publications, Inc.
All rights reserved
First printing 1989, Spring Publications, Inc.,
P. O. Box 222069, Dallas, TX 75222
Printed in the United States of America
Text on acidfree paper
Cover designed by Margot McLean
The image: Marcel Broodthaers, *Chaise lilas avec oeufs*
(Lilac Chair with Eggs), 1966, private collection
Photograph courtesy of the Walker Art Center, Minneapolis,
exhibition *Marcel Broodthaers*

International distributors:
Spring; Postfach; 8803 Rüschlikon; Switzerland.
Japan Spring Sha, Inc.; 12–10, 2-Chome,
Nigawa Takamaru; Takarazuka 665, Japan.
Element Books Ltd; Longmead Shaftesbury;
Dorset SP7 8PL; England.
Astam Books Pty. Ltd.; 162–168 Parramatta Road;
Stanmore N.S.W. 2048; Australia.
Libros e Imagenes; Apdo. Post 40–085;
México D.F. 06140; México.
Zipak Livraria Editora Ltda; Alameda Lorena 871;
01424 Sao Paulo SP; Brazil.

Library of Congress Cataloging-in-Publication Data
Broodmales.
    p.   cm.
Reprint, with new introd. (2nd work). Originally published:
Manchester, Eng.   :   Manchester University Press, 1929.
Includes bibliographical references.
Contents: A psychological essay on men in childbirth / Nor Hall —
The custom of couvade / Warren R. Dawson.
ISBN 0–88214–340–9 (alk. paper)
1. Couvade.   2. Birth customs.   3. Men—Psychology.
4. Childbirth—Psychology.   I. Hall, Nor. Psychological essay on
men in childbirth.   1989.   II. Dawson, Warren R. (Warren Royal),
1888–   Custom of couvade.   1989.
GT2460.B75   1989
392'.12—dc20                          89–21777
                                            CIP

# CONTENTS

# ILLUSTRATIONS

# ACKNOWLEDGMENTS

LYNNE Ballew translated the Greek and Latin passages and Margie Goggans the French (see Appendix).

"As in the Old Days" by Robert Duncan, *Bending the Bow*. Copyright © 1968 by Robert Duncan. Reprinted by permission of New Directions Publishing Corporation.

The Sorrowful god or thinker of Hamangia reproduced from Marija Gimbutas, *The Goddesses and Gods of Old Europe* (London: Thames and Hudson), by permission of the author.

Dionysos with his mystic alter ego, on a krater by the Altamura painter. Ferrara, Museo Archeologico Nazionale. Reproduced from C. Kerényi, *Dionysos: Archetypal Image of Indestructible Life* (Princeton: Princeton University Press, 1976).

Christ with breasts, reproduced from C. H. Cahier, S. J., *Des Saints dans Part Populaire* (Paris, 1867).

Buddha with Buddha in belly, a woodcut by Lu K'uan Yü, reproduced from *Taoist Yoga: Alchemy and Immortality* (London: Century Hutchinson Limited).

How the husband assists in the birth of a child, Guadalupe, widow of Ramon Medina Silva, after a yarn painting by Ramon, reproduced by permission of the Fine Arts Museums of San Francisco, gift of Peter F. Young.

# A Psychological Essay on Men in Childbirth

## NOR HALL

# PREFACE

WARREN Royal Dawson's booklined study sat squarely on the prime meridian of nineteenth-century social anthropology, where scholars of antiquity had recently been introduced to investigators of living cultures. The nature of "the study of Mankind" was dramatically affected by this meeting of minds, and Dawson was in the forefront of the research it generated. In his work on the male birth-related customs of couvade, he refers to his role in this new enterprise of cultural studies as map-making. The Englishman born in 1888 mapped what he considered to be "the eccentricities of the human mind" as manifest in the spread of a "strange" tendency for native men to imitate the woman in childbed.

By day Dawson was an insurance underwriter and by night a self-educated Egyptologist who concentrated on lifting tales from parchment. He spent innumerable hours in the back halls of the British Museum—first under the tutelage of Sir Wallis Budge and later on his own. He compensated for what he thought to be a deplorable lack of formal education by producing a mountain of work. He wrote the classic text on mummification, several biographies of noted anthropologists, compiled the still current *Who Was Who in Egyptology*, and functioned as honorary librarian for established insti-

3

tutions including Lloyd's of London, the Medical
Society of London, the Linnean Society, and for the
Huxley papers in the Imperial College of Science. He
was a man consummately interested in documenta-
tion.

At the time when Dawson and his mentors
labored as classical scholars, proponents of "open
air anthropology" began to speak out, urging the
researcher of cultures to change his position.
Bronislaw Malinowski, for example, at a gathering
to honor their teacher Sir James Frazer (author of
the twelve-volume *Golden Bough*) argued against
"hear-say note taking." He implored the anthropologist to "go out to visit the villages, settle in pile
dwellings, work with the natives in their gardens,
sail with them to distant sandbanks. Fish, trade, and
talk with them."[1] His was a strong voice in the call
to relinquish the position in the study or on the
veranda. "Put down your whiskey and soda, and go
down the steps into the field."

It is unlikely that Dawson, who disdained social
activities and avoided sporting pastimes to opt for
more leisure time with letters and papyri, took many
such drinks. Nonetheless he had never been into the
field. Anthropologists did not do field work originally, but relied on reports of adventurers. Likewise
archaeologists before this era taught on the basis of
"excavating" classical literature. We wonder, therefore, what Dawson thought when he heard these in-

---

[1] *The Frazer Lectures 1922–1932*, ed. W. R. Dawson (Freeport,
New York: Books for Libraries Press, 1967). Malinowski contributed
the lecture "Myth in Primitive Psychology." Quotes from the *Lectures*
are his and Edward Westermark's in the chapter on "The Study of
Popular Sayings."

junctions to change. As collator and editor of these varied opinions for the book called *The Frazer Lectures 1922–1932*, he must have lived intensely in the debate. Collegial love for Frazer brought out strong defenses of the armchair anthropologist: "A commander should not expose himself to the dangers attending action in the field." Another voice, probably closer to the Dawson described as sending out friendly queries and expecting answers by return post, stressed the necessity of both positions saying that the anthropologist's study is a rallying point for scattered thoughts and evidence. According to this picture, the man in the study busily propounds questions for the man in the field who sends in the evidence to revise the question, etc.

These earnest debates about where exactly the observer of mankind should be situated were conducted by the white man who sadly made that which he desired to see vanish before his very eyes. Dawson noted this tendency of the custom "to disappear before the influence of the white man," but by this he meant that the primitive traditions went away prior to the coming of civilization. He could not see from the perspective of Ivan Illich, for example, writing *Gender* in 1982, who says that male ethnographers (and their competitive female colleagues) fed their model informants (i.e., men) to male interlocutors who elicited responses to suit. Women were not ideal informants because they giggled when young, snorted when old, rejected questions, and laughed at the researchers' proposals. Illich's point is that the student of gender-related information must employ an explicitly non-scientific mode of inquiry that proceeds indirectly with metaphor to get at what is otherwise elusive, muted, and unperceived.[1]

Dawson's studies, other than his collation of couvade material, were not gender-related. He relied on concrete remnants rather than on informants to write the museum's exhibition catalog of human remains. His work on mummies and tattooing and the magico-medicinal use of leeches, for example, was based more on artifact than oral tradition. He was a devotee of a school of thought that believed in the ultimate Egyptian origin of civilization. The reach of civilization could thus be tracked from the Nile Valley to the Indian Ocean to Western China according to the found evidence of practices like mummification, ear-piercing, and cranial deformation. This fantasy of geographical diffusion that uses bones and artifacts as trace elements also organizes his study of the living customs of couvade. His chapter mapping the distribution of the practice around the world reads in a chantlike way reminiscent of Allen Ginsberg's poem of the breath exhaled in meditation. It wafts around the planet, from Colorado mountain top to San Francisco Bay through the slums of Shanghai, before returning for the inhalation. ("Mindbreaths")

"The Custom of Couvade" is extremely thorough, ascribed, and careful not to be insightful. Fidelity to Truth makes Dawson bring differing opinions together on a single page, but the pages remain weighted by his conviction that the irrational cannot be explained and that the importance of his project is in documenting the stamp and spread of a strange custom. He doesn't exactly dismiss the students

[1] *Gender* (New York: Random House, 1982), pp. 128–30.

of couvade who would attempt seeing "into" the customs, like Crawley and Westermark, who raise questions about the nature of intimacy, but he places their comments to fall in left field. They would open the interpretive range of the research to include the woman's point of view as well as questions about the concept of fatherhood. Both the woman-path and the father-nature-path lead close to the lair of Dawson's disputants who favor a "theory of independent origins." In opposition to Dawson and the diffusionists, they posit a universality in human nature which would allow for human beings to come up with ways of acting the same without their ancestors ever having met.

The independent origin idea takes more stock in the interior. It wants to speculate about human nature, instinct, or the psyche. It suggests that there are similarities in the human experience that make it occur to men on both sides of the Pacific to participate in the process of a woman's pregnancy by going into a secluded hut where they are not permitted to touch their own bodies. Dawson refrains from inquiring into this image with any interest in its interiority, yet does the exhaustive work of providing his readers, of whatever school, with a catalog of critical details. Rich images of what happens to a man in couvade can be lifted out of the couch of his theory like a string of hieroglyphics and examined one by one for the imaginal insights they contain. Patterns tend to emerge. The man in the hut who is "out of touch" appears in an adjacent "glyph" standing by a pool of water. Nearby a nurse figure—is it male or female?—reclines in a hammock holding an infant.

The eye of the archaeologist deciphers these images as if they are archaic, belonging to the remote past, and not as archetypal—which would mean admitting the tug of the contents on his own soul. Dawson is influenced enough by the new anthropology of his time to look around and see a remnant of couvade in modern England. But he takes the remnant idea literally by looking for evidence in the outermost (i.e., less civilized) British Isles, rather than trying to discern traces of the couvade in men around him. When psychology enters the discussion, it would extend the anthropological field theory in all directions including the territory designated "within," to ask not only what the living customs have meant to other men and women, but also to ask what the evidence wants with us now.

# BROODMALES

A CONGOLESE Bantu sits stone still in front of his expectant wife's hut. All the cords and knots of his clothes have been cut so that when he rises he will be as naked as the child coming in.[1] "Hatch as hatch can," as James Joyce says. This is how the father does it.

To make its way into the world, new life needs an opening. Infancy wants a tender reception. The man who goes to lie in the hammock next to the hut makes a receptive curve of himself to welcome the child. He unties knots and cords, opens doors and windows, unbraids hair, frees tethered animals, unfastens the moored boat. Everything bound up is freed so that energy can flow. This release is especially critical at the time of birth. Things need to be undone. The father needs not to go about business as usual, needs not to get things done, but rather to leave work undone, to brood rather than be busy.

In the beginning the Spirit of God "brooded over the face of the deep" in order to bring the first day out of darkness into light. As a great bird would hatch a cosmic egg, the Spirit settled its intent upon

---

[1] All of the references to specific couvade customs, unless otherwise noted in the text, are from Dawson's essay following.

9

that which was not-yet-created. Such settling of intent upon us is often prelude to a creative emergence. To be brooded over is to be completely covered by an extraordinary concentration of warmth that waits for the slightest stirring in the depths. It is a gathering of energy that is nonforceful even though it has purpose. Its purpose is not to penetrate—which is unusual for the spirit regarded as masculine—but to bring forth. This intention to bring forth is powerful in the way of roiling black thunderheads gathering electricity to themselves or those majestic laboring clouds of Milton's that rest upon the mountain's breast. Brood force is as intense as the storming God and as soft as the underbelly of a hen. It is very heavy, but will not break an egg.

A mother with this brood awareness knows when a sleeping child stirs to the need of cover. The body so recently come from her own, where covering was accomplished merely by the child's dwelling *in utero*, feels like an extension of herself. A father, likewise, in the beginning, needs to spread himself out as if spreading his wings for cover (rather than for flight). Ainu fathers in northern Japan sit wrapped and still by the fire in the same room with the newborn. The brood male conserves his heat to pass it on to his child. Couvade customs recognize that children need warmth from their fathers, especially small children who need to be covered because they cannot take cover. They need to be brooded over, surrounded by thoughts, enveloped by the heart's heat, made the focus of concentrated energy that is not invasive. Our language locates the feeling of "cherishing" in the Old English *bredan* which means "to actively warm" or "direct the heat of the body towards."

Brooding turns ominous when it hovers without cherishing—as in the cases where fathers hurt their wives and children. Brooding turns morbid when it loses its object. Someone in a "brown study," for example—or shades deeper, a "black mood"—is so self-absorbed that his energy concentrates into an impenetrable field. Dark brooding establishes distance between people regardless of proximity. Roland Barthes describes that blackening of mood that will occur in relationships as "a faint black intoxication." The cloud that moves over the landscape of two of us is the thought "I am missing something."[1] It is another covert symptom of couvade reported by women who sense their partner's emotional absence increase in proportion to their pregnancy. In these cases 'the object lost' to the darkly brooding man is his wife. She is lost to him because her energy has shifted into the brooding mode that has internal life (i.e., rather than his life) as constant focus.

Recent studies of the father's role in all aspects of childbirth identify four possible directions for his "pregnancy career" to take.[2] In one, he denies the pregnancy, abandons the woman, and leaves to establish an alternate identity. In the second, he regards the pregnancy as his wife's responsibility and his place as peripheral. He may help if asked. Third,

---

[1] From "Clouds" in *A Lover's Discourse* (New York: Hill and Wang, 1979), pp. 169–70.

[2] See the article "Fatherhood: The Social Construction of Pregnancy and Birth," by J. Richman and W. O. Goldthorp in *The Place of Birth* (New York: Oxford University Press, 1978), p. 168.

the father develops a special bond with the foetus and shares the pregnancy experience. And fourth, he claims total identification with the foetus, sometimes to the exclusion of the mother's role, and attempts to cut her off from everyday activities.

Boundaries between these possibilities blur a bit in the psyche where no man's repertoire is limited to a single part. The fact that customs of couvade seem to chart a man's course through a continuum of involvement represented by these too distinct, yet recognizable, roles suggests that we read between the lines to discern the arc of a plot. Most men will know the feeling of each of these courses at different times, in either their wives' pregnancies or as partner to their own creative process.

Couvade customs that are enacted primarily at the birth of the first child have as their aim the preparation of the man for becoming a father. Once he goes through the structural shift that thoroughly rearranges his sense of himself around a child's soul, he who was separate is no longer. Observances in the first stage of pregnancy require that a man give up his ordinary activities. In order to learn how to brood in the woman's way, he is cut off from the male world. He lays his hatchet in the arm of a tree and sticks his hunting spears into the ground. He can no longer be careless. If he fishes, someone else has to make the hooks or his child might have a harelip. If he is a builder, another man must drive the stakes into the soil. All violent moves, including riding a horse too hard, jumping from rooftop to rooftop, or climbing rocks, are to be avoided. Is it because such actions "cause" miscarriage as Dawson's anthropologists report, or is it that the deliberate, daily exercise of care on the part of the father perceptibly attunes him to the body as carrier?

Girls learn by hearsay that they might miscarry if they ride a horse hard, jump from a rooftop, etc. They would also know, if open to the primitive wisdom of resemblance, that driving a stake into the earth is an imaginal abortion procedure. To ensure safe carriage of the child in her womb, a woman avoids acts of violence. To carry it in her heart she avoids images of violence that feel potentially harmful to the envelopment of the embryo. If her consideration for the internal environment contributes to its being carried in comfort, then the parallel considerations of the one beside her would serve to further extend the field of safety for the unborn.

This is not so much causal thinking—or superstitious and stupid as some observers stated—but rather a deeply systemic point of view that shaped communal life: where one member suffers, the other suffers also. When a stillbirth occurs, the father's intemperance could be blamed. In an example from Paraguay, the women's accusations run thus:

> You swam across the chilly river,
> You loaded your stomach with water hog,
> You devoured underground honey,
> You stamped the bees with your feet,
> You did not abstain from drink,
> You rode so long that you sweated and grew tired.

Their message is "You did not care." Taking care, in order of accusation, would mean keeping warm, being moderate, non-invasive, gentle, clear, steady, and conservative of energy—all characteristics of an attentive state of fatherhood. His training toward fatherhood is supposed to keep step with the gradual changes occurring to the woman who can no longer regard her life or her body as her own.

Where couvade consciousness occurs, men's pregnancy careers collapse into the third route primarily—of developing the foetal bond. But the impulse to abandon of the first route and the reluctant participation of the second are likely to occur as earlier stages in the pregnancy process. The fourth course, of total identification with the foetus to the exclusion of the mother's role, also appears in customs where men enact the scene of being born and are received and wrapped by attendants. The effect of this sympathetic action is to relieve pain for mother and child. But the shady side of sympathy is power, and in a culture where men have no mentors to guide their involvement, attempts to act sympathetically can tip over into destructive control. John Lennon, for instance, so identified with the foetus that he made Yoko Ono sit in a wheelchair all day to be pushed around the apartment. He stopped smoking and using drugs for a moment in time, but was so overbearing—monitoring her diet, putting her to bed, taking her to the bathroom—that she upped her smoking to four packs a day.

A woman slips naturally into the image of total identification because the child so slowly becomes her body. Most of us do not free our children (or our creations) as quickly as the Aztec mother who cuts the umbilical cord with a flint stone saying: "I cut from your middle the navel string. . . . Here you sprout, here you flower. Here you are severed from

your mother as the chip is struck from the stone."
We tend to hold on to the umbilical closeness that
makes us one. A new mother inseparable from her
infant and on the edge of collapse hands her baby to
her husband saying, "here, hold me a while. . . ."
The mother, like the child with whom she is still
completely identified, wants to be held by a man
who can sit "and hatch new myths by the log road."
(Gary Snyder)

The social construction of fatherhood in a post-
Christian era does not allow men to sit around.
How many pictures of Joseph with the child sitting
on his lap have you ever seen?

Sitting (like a hen), brooding, covering, incubating, hatching are all properties of hens rather
than cocks. Customs of couvade imprint cock-
culture with patterns of typically female behavior.
The aboriginal practice of penile sub-incision is a
literal example. Men operate on the penis to make it
resemble a vulva. Its bleeding is then likened to the
potent blood of menses (potent because it can make
children), and the wound is called "woman."[1] Trac-
ing this line back even further to neolithic cave
sculpture, Michael Ventura notes the patterns in
bone carving of "the Goddess tattooing herself onto
the maleness of men."[2] His reverie begins at an in-
tersection by the sea in Santa Monica where the
modern sculpture of the city's namesake clearly
resembles a phallus. Her minimalist woman form
fills out a granite erection in a larger piece than the

[1] Bruno Bettelheim, *Symbolic Wounds* (London: Thames and Hudson, 1955), p. 177.

[2] *Shadow Dancing in the U.S.A.* (Los Angeles: Jeremy P. Tarcher,
1985). See essay called "Notes on Three Erections," pp. 29–32.

archaic fragments that have been found in caves. Nonetheless, the impulse that claims the male member as female appears similar.

In practicing couvade, the male makes himself wombly. An initiated aboriginal man made womanly by sub-incision can imitate the womb's ability to open. Zeus, in the mythology of the Mediterranean, opened his own thigh in order to carry his unborn son. He did it with the loud cry of the father ringing out: "O Come child, enter this my male womb!"[1] Then he bore the child God Dionysos in this makeshift prenatal chamber which he closed with golden clasps.

A child emerging from such a father hold is called "twice born"—once from the mother and once from the father. As is the convention in patriarchal Christianity, the mother is mortal, of the earth and matter, and the father is immortal, belonging to the realm of overhead, "heavenly" bodies and metaphor. Tradition has it that one part needs to be grounded and the other lifted. In other eras it is the man who is grounded and the woman elevated. Either way, the child borne by the awareness of both is designated special, gifted, divine—a child of Earth and Starry Sky.

Young god-likeness in anyone benefits from the embrace of an elder who knows the ways of another gender in his own body. Tiresias the blind seer could see what others could not because he was man-womanly. Paposilenus (another name for Bacchus) was the teacher of Dionysos at an early age when the boy was dressed and raised as a girl. Paunchy and

[1] Jane Ellen Harrison, *Themis: A Study of the Social Origins of Greek Religion* (New York: Meridian, 1962), p. 34.

weighted with milk-giving paps, he nourished the girlishness in the boy with his babble. Spurting milk, wine, honey, poetry and music, he was a fount of liquid wisdom in a state of ready "let down" (as in the milk-filled breast of the mother). To the man made womanly, this sweetness mixes with his sweat to sustain, even "endow," the child.

Basque men lie down with their newborns who find their initial shelter against the father's chest. Absorbing the first post-natal sweat from the father ensures the incorporation of elemental humors from both parents. The mingling of moisture, like the mingling of breath, enwraps the two as one from inside. The certainty that infants need nursing care from both parents is represented in the Basque father's lying in and in the Brahman's ritual of giving his finger dipped in milk and honey to the child to suck. Actual nursing through the rare development of male mammary glands is possible, but the symbolic gesture is much more common and often regarded as necessary for the well-being, body and soul, of the child.

Father nursing is not simply a usurpation of woman's natural role. One of his nursing modes, artificial feeding, has thousands of years of history behind it. Feeding horns with holes in the end and clay vessels with miniature rounded spouts for sucking were used in pre-dynastic Egypt and in fifteenth-century Iceland, for example, to feed infants whose mother died or who had physical deformations that made sucking impossible.[1] In her research on the history of infant feeding, Valerie Fildes suggests that

[1] Valerie Fildes, *Breasts, Bottles, and Babies* (Edinburgh: Edinburgh University Press, 1986), p. 264.

it might also have been a means for peasant women to return quickly to the fields. Mothers who could not or would not breastfeed (and here the negative influence of the man is felt in the dictation of nursing fashion) usually used a wet nurse or left the handrearing of children to other women. A child raised "by hand" is raised by artifice rather than "by breast." When the father played this role it was ritualized, which is to say his enactment of nursing served a necessity other than biological.

Breastfeeding bonds are so strong that even thinking of the child will stimulate the let down of a mother's milk. Nursing mothers "hear" their babies cry when they are miles apart and immediately begin to flow. When they are close, but sleeping, a mother's REM (rapid eye movement) cycles when dreaming occurs are organized unconsciously to end when the infant rouses. Recognizing the extent to which the two are tied in and knowing that this was collective knowledge, the prophet Isaiah took this image of care and gave it to God who said He remembered his bond to his people even more certainly than the most certain: "Can a woman forget her sucking child. . . . Even they may forget, yet I will not forget you." (49:15) This God who broods and groans when creating also gives men breasts. The prophet's image for ultimate revolution in the Kingdom is that the Lord God will turn the oppressors into nursing fathers. (Is. 49:22)

The necessity, then, is that a man feel the swell and fullness of lactation and its sweet release according to the need of the other. Thoughts of her child, or even of anonymous children in the news, will make a mother's breasts sting long after she's stopped nursing. It is similar to the way a heart can ache or eyes smart on behalf of another. A father with this kind of feeling "fosters" (as in "feeds") his child out of himself, knowing, as a mother does, that all the needs of the child in this moment are within his capacity to fill. We know that this desire has inhabited the imagination of men for generations because of the accounts of Amazon tribes in the ancient world. Johannes Boemmus, reporting in 1555, retells the story of the warrior women handing their babes over to men kept for the purpose of handrearing: "The children as soon as they were borne, were delivered to the men to nourysshe up with milke, and such other things as they're tendrenes required. . . ."[1]

The involvement of the father of Dionysos starts with the moment called "quickening." It is that instant of first feeling life registered as movement. A mother experiences quickening as an initial flutter or a tiny fish-like flick against the bank of the womb. It makes your heart skip a beat. Or you hold your breath to make a space for the immensity of significance registered suddenly in that smallest of gestures. Its occurrence is deeply internal and protected from view, yet the feeling marks the beginning of sweeping changes on the face of life. The father's song of quickening encourages the leap of embryonic life. Zeus's song to his in-dwelling son sounds less like a prayer or praise song than an injunction, a command for life to spring forth into fullness and productivity. The father recognizes the deeply hidden movement as critical. If that initial jump start does not occur in the darkness, then

[1] Quoted in Fildes, p. 262. From Boemmus's *Fardle of Facions*.

nothing will come to light. Consequently, the father ordains the quickening:

> Leap, Child, for full jars,
> Leap for fleecy flocks,
> Leap for fields of fruit and for hives to bring increase,
> Leap for our cities,
> Leap for our seaborne ships, for our young citizens,
>     and for goodly Themis.[1]

He is invoking a vision of abundance to fill the full spectrum from mother nature's realm of bees, sheep, and preserves to the jurisdiction of Themis, Goddess of rightly ordered civilized life. A "leap" is a quick and decisive increase which is the father's essential wish for all that is his.

The Zeusian fantasy of childraising continues with the God's enlisting a wild group of boys called the shielded nurturers (Kouretes). These youths are his attendants, nurses for the child born as "Lord of All Wet and Gleaming." They hide him from enemies with noise of beating feet and the mad, distracting clash of swords and shields. They are noisemakers, evil dispellers, and nourishers in the manner of initiators who provide information mana. Once they've tricked the child away into seclusion by confusing its guardian with drums and din, they raise it in the secret ways of youths who are full of a God's divine charge. This means that the boy child learns to identify with the gnosis of the Father (Jesus at twelve saying, "I and the Father are One") and refuses to acknowledge the maternal body that bore him.

[1] *Themis*, p. 8.

Initiation into manhood requires this temporary disavowal of the biological mother. It is comparable, in a general way, to a girl's initiation into the bear cub pack of the Goddess Artemis. During their pubescent years in the wilderness between the ages of nine and fourteen, Artemis's saffron-robed cubs see no boys or men. For youths of any gender this protected time of indeterminacy between childhood and adulthood is needed for finding the God, or the myth, or the power that claims them. This lineage claims their soul alongside the earthly rights of physical parentage.

Some wise cultures allow for a gender-crossed claim. Not all boys want to belong to Zeus or his counterpart. For example, Plains Indian boys play a Fire Throwing Game where the young warriors throw live coals in mudballs at each other and fight with burning sticks. The peacefully inclined boy who does not want to take the warrior path has an alternative. He may be chosen as a *berdache*, a man who will live in-between what is regarded as manly and womanly.[1] Such a boy among the Papago would take the brushfire test to determine his future. He would be placed in the center of a dense circle of brush with a pack strap and bow. The circle is then set on fire. If he comes running out with the woman's pack strap, he would henceforth be respectfully seen as burdened with the spiritual responsibilities of the *berdache* who dresses and acts like a woman.

Yielding to the desire to experience womanliness in the body is a hidden essential to male culture.

[1] Walter L. Williams, *The Spirit and the Flesh: Sexual Diversity in American Indian Culture* (Boston: Beacon, 1968), p. 48.

Myths give cosmic permission for the reversal—not only the Greek, but the Basque and the Celtic as well. Zeus accomplished it, the *berdache* do it. And men's dreams point the way for individuals to undertake the mother reclamation at specific times in life. A young man who is terminally ill, for example, finds his lost babies in the driveway and picks them up to nurse them. After the resistance to identification with the Mother that characterizes a young man's initiation rites comes the ironic reversal of preparation for fatherhood: he must locate mother in his own body.

Post-Dawson anthropologists have noted that the cultures they observe seem to need a certain amount of role exchange.[1] Men need either to act out their own fantasy of being within a woman body, or they need other men to enact it on their behalf. As a result, there is virtually no evidence of couvade where transvestites are recognized and given a respected place among their people. Couvade is practiced most extensively in cultures that give men no other way of being female. In our current global village where gender enactments are less obviously circumscribed by consensual tradition, we are more free to try on the role of the other.

But simply reversing the parts (father stays home, mother goes to work) gets us nowhere. This freedom that is only skin-deep needs to sink deeper into the body. Men and women can exchange roles, but if that which is regarded as the province of the female remains devalued, the couvade impulse is forced into hiding. For example, if a woman is sup-

[1] R.L. Munroe, "Male Transvestism and the Couvade: A Psycho-Cultural Analysis," *Ethos* 8 (1980): 53.

posed to go right on working through her first trimester fatigue "just like a man," a man has little chance of participating in her withdrawal from activity.[1] His covert desire to participate turns into depression. If incubation and a reflective turning-in-on-oneself are not valued phases of pregnancy even for the woman, a man, unconsciously participating, will suffer stomach aches and have back trouble. If a woman is not supposed to trust the internal moon clock of her uterus because the doctor insists on a Caesarean section for his convenience, a husband has no chance of learning the tissue-deep patience that waits for something, especially new life, to emerge in its own time.

How then, when birth time comes, does a man recognize mother in his own body? First he goes through a necessary period of being out of touch. He is out of touch with other men. He is out of touch with his woman. He is even out of touch with his physical self. All because he is to be the site of a major transformation. In Papua New Guinea when a woman is about to give birth, the man goes into five days of seclusion during which time he is required to be out of touch with his body, in a sense, by following strict taboos. He has to scratch himself with a stick, eat food with a spoon, and roll tobacco with an implement so that his hands do not touch it. His contamination is related to the encroachment of the woman mystery (of birth) that promises to radically alter his existence. His seclusion is silent and has to be patient because the moment of

[1] See the piece on expectant men by Michael Finley, "Couvade: Cloud of Unknowing," *Clinton Street Quarterly* (Summer, 1988).

emergence is not up to him. As it says at the end of *Finnegans Wake*, "All's silent, and set for restart."

A man whose inner circuits are suffering this critical re-routing appears broody, quiet, out of touch, "not promising"—a condition expressed in the word *despondent*, meaning "away from promise." Despondency wants a sponsor, which is what happens in the next phase. In *Pilgrim's Progress*, the pilgrim meets a figure called Help only when he reaches the Slough of Despond.

The man in the set-apart Papuan hut meets an elder who will be his sponsor. This elder has to be a father. He comes to take the young man to the edge of the water, by a pool where a small leaf-house has been constructed for him. It is decorated with a profusion of red flowers and leafy bundled herbs. Here he is instructed to drink from the aromatic pool and bathe in its fragrant waters. After the cleansing he must dive to the bottom to retrieve a large white ring-like object. We don't know what this circle means to him. It could be emblematic of continuity like the ouroboric round. Olive Schreiner (who wrote *Woman and Labor*) would say it represents the cervical os that shapes the head size and thus the intelligence and future of everyman. Margaret Mead wonders if his getting "the phallic eel" signifies the retrieval of masculinity after his participation in the feminine realm of having a baby.[1] In any case the ring forms a closed parenthesis around his boyhood.

The sponsor has to be a man who has known

[1] *Sex and Temperament* (New York: William Morrow and Company, 1963), p. 35.

something of the female mystery, who has passed through the lean-to of flowers. (In primitive Orphic rites it was called "going through the hoops"—of flowers.) He has been perfumed and blessed, has taken the herbal drink and gone under. He has enacted the experience of loss and retrieval under the watchful eye of an elder, who, in his turn, had gone through it.

Boys flounder when there are no sponsors. They also tend to grow into the trap of the first described "pregnancy career"—of abandoning the woman to establish a different identity—when they have not gone through a natural separation from mother. If they haven't distanced themselves from her to link up with their own soul's lineage, then they are likely to feel compelled to go for it by leaving the mothers of their own children. It's bad timing. And increasingly problematic, but the old stories tell us that the kind of masculinity that can experience weakening by participating in the submission of pregnancy and labor—i.e., the man who can be flat on his back on behalf of the birth process—has already gone through the field of resistance to the mother. We see boys sporting all around us on this field: they push away from the lap of mother in exaggerated imitation of the preferred male image by swearing, swaggering, acting tough, being cruel, never crying. They often become young men who are more interested in how hard they can be and in how long this hardness can be maintained than they are, or ever will be, in the soft belly condition of the Buddha.

Maturity is marked by a wound that weakens a man's gender identification. Angela Carter's postmodern novel *The Passion of New Eve*, set underground in an apocalyptic American Southwest takes the archetypal thigh wounds of Zeus and the Arthurian heroes and deepens them with the aid of the black mother surgeon's blade. Her male protagonist Evelyn is transformed into Eve whose wound becomes a womb that bleeds at the bidding of the moon. More than that it becomes a source of pleasure and, eventually, the site of conception.

Christ bore a wound that made him female at the age of thirty-three. The wound in his side was regarded as a womb by the slightly blood-obsessed Count Ludwig von Zinzendorf in the Moravian community of Bethlehem, Pennsylvania, in the 1700s.[1] He ordered a niche constructed in the wall of the church to be lined with red cloth to make it resemble the wound in Christ's side. He called it the "birthplace." Out of it "all souls were 'dug' or born," so he placed baptized infants in the red hole and then removed them as if delivering them out of the womb of the Church. These children were the twice born: "born again" from the wound in His side. The poet, standing at the niche, writes,

> I am
> at the lips before speech, at life's
> labia, Her crack of a door opening,
> her cunt a wound now
> the gash in His side
> from which monthly blood flows •
> so Zinzendorf saw,
> all maidens bear Christ's sign with them

[1] Jacob John Sessler, *Communal Pietism among the Early American Moravians* (New York: H. Holt and Co., 1933), p. 150.

THE SORROWFUL GOD OR, THINKER OF HAMANGIA

DIONYSOS WITH HIS MYSTIC ALTER EGO

CHRIST WITH BREASTS

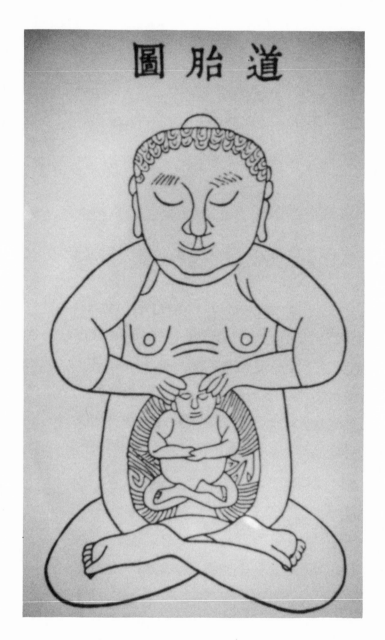

圖 胎 道

BUDDHA WITH BUDDHA IN BELLY

> •    at this flowing
> souls gather[1]    •

A man wounded in midlife becomes suddenly like a maiden—subject to flowing. Iron John, who is a central figure in Robert Bly's work on fairy tales for men, suffers the female stroke at the end of his lance-led adventures. He rears up on his magnificent steed. His golden hair falls down. His thigh is cut. So the one who has arrived arrives wounded, and the damaged one is made complete in the flash of steel that leaves him open.

Some say the thigh wound is a visual echo of the ripe sun's wound as it gets cut going down over the western horizon. Mature men are often more attractive precisely because they have moved beyond the height of potency. You can't look at the sun at noon. There is no room for a woman in a constantly erect male body. The wound signifies opening, softening, and weakening. When the sun's light weakens, the different light of the moon shows with more strength and clarity. The weakening meant here is the diminishment of difference that certain customs of couvade make their aim. Men are starved on restricted diets, made to lie down all day, deprived of stimulants and exercise to weaken them to the point of needing attendants. Their own provider's persona slips away when they are reduced to watching life in passing from a pallet. Depending on the timing of his weakening, the man's state is sympathetically helpful to the woman or to the newborn. When she is in labor, he will lie covered under a

[1] Robert Duncan, "As in the Old Days—Passages 8," in *Bending the Bow* (London: Jonathan Cape Limited, 1971), pp. 24–25.

piece of her clothing to transfer the sweats, sounds, and contractions of labor to himself.

When the child is born, the couvade father assists by essentially collapsing into its field: lying prone, fed, treated, washed, dressed, and visited, the man feels the welcome surrounding the newborn. He lies with the child until the cord falls off. He becomes the child's nurse so that the mother can go back to her work. He stays in bed with the baby to receive the blessings of other family members. Marco Polo saw a man in Chinese Turkestan who stayed in bed with his child for forty days. "Forty days and forty nights" rings in the biblical ear as the time of the Great Flood when God wiped out all that had been and restored "the deep" so that he could begin again. In the Basque mythology of creation the brooding of the male God Aitor is also attached to this moment. At the time of the deluge, Aitor and his wife sought refuge on the summit of the highest mountain surrounded by thundering impenetrable darkness. She gave birth in the cave and then went out in search of food. Her child's cries echoed in the cavern making her fearful that a wild beast would hear and come to snatch the little one away. So she asked Aitor to lie on the bed of skins and hold the child in his great arms.

The bard singing this Epic of Aitor in the year 241, on the occasion of celebrating peace between Rome and Carthage, said that the sons of Aitor take to childbed as soon as the woman rises. They lie down, with respect for their ancestors, to pass on the manly breath which the child inhales for strength. This way the child is in-spired by its father. Perhaps the breath dries the newborn as in the poet's

words, "Dry me with your breath. / For intense
breath is prayer, / and it loosens the bonds of water."
(Bly, "A Dream about Sam")

Tribal culture conspired to create an occasion for
the birth of the father. As his wife's pregnancy pro-
gressed and he made himself increasingly scarce in
men's circles, gradually stopped working, and laid
down the weapons of hunt and war, his actions
became increasingly focused on the details of tender
life. He would change the way he walked, taking
care not to snap twigs (in the exact same way our
children avoid cracks on the sidewalk—"step on a
crack, break your mother's back," "step on a line,
make it all fine"). The man practicing couvade consciousness would construct a little bridge over any
stream he came to cross, even a rivulet. Or, he
would bend a leaf into the shape of a boat for his
small companion.

His careful moves through the ordinary world
were directed by an acute awareness of the vulner-
able childspirit that might follow him. For a while
he must not go into scary places. If, in the first week
of the child's life he has to go any distance, he will
bring a little stone back with him, place it by the
door when he arrives, call out "Come here," and
then wait until the child sneezes. He captures the
soul in the stone and takes it back in to the child saying, "Here, I brought your soul back." By various
accounts, men give soul, backbone, kindliness, and
face to their children.

Margaret Mead tells the story of how the Arapesh couple "have babies together."[1] Their verb "to
bear" is used indiscriminately of either man or

---

[1] *Sex and Temperament*, pp. 32–36.

woman. After the child is born, the father lies down with the mother and child and is described as having a baby. He bears the child with the woman so that they can give it a life-soul. This is the same as giving it a face. Facial resemblance later in life tells which parent gave the soul. Finding one's face and losing it is a familiar motif to dream-workers. Not having a face or having a face blurred into imprecision may be related to the lack of this close father looking at you. When fathers are absent, children wander unensouled. From the Arapesh perspective they are likely to be isolated, somber, and ignorant of their own names. After birth they say a mother and father can walk about freely, but the baby cannot go out until it laughs up into its father's face. Then the child is given its name and taken out to meet the world.

Myths make it clear that men who do not understand this necessity of "having a baby" with their women stand to lose ground in drastic measure. A Celtic tale called "The Pangs of Ulster" circles the absence of sympathy and settles a curse on the thoughtless husband. It begins in the home of a well-to-do Irish countryman whose wife has just died. One day a mysterious, fine-looking woman enters his house as if she belongs there. She settles things into place with care and makes the household work well with no want for anything. When the time comes round for the Ulster fair, the man (now her husband) sets out. She suggests that he take care not to grow boastful in things he might say. "That isn't likely," he replies.

Later, at the end of the festive day, the king's horses were brought out onto the field. People began to murmur that nothing could beat those horses.

The careless man spoke up to announce, "My wife is faster," so of course she was sent for immediately. When the messenger arrived, she told him it would be a heavy burden for her to race to free her husband because she was full with child. The insistent man said, "Burden? Your husband will die unless you come." So she went and pleaded again before the crowd, "A mother bore every one of you! Help me! The race must wait!" But the king and the crowd were unmoved. She stood furiously radiant and solemn in that moment and said that for this wrong done to her they would suffer a greater. "Who are you?" the king asked. "I am called Macha, the daughter of the Stranger, son of the Ocean. Make ready your horses!"

A deep shudder would have passed through the crowd at the name of Macha—Goddess of the galloping horse and the race of heartbeats in women's labor. The race began even as her labor pains began. And when the king's chariot reached the winning post she was there already, giving birth to twins beneath the heads of the panting steeds. At the very moment of delivery she screamed out that all who heard her cry would be seized in their times of greatest difficulty with these very pains of childbirth, every man for four days and five nights.

This affliction, called "the enchantment of Macha," carried on for nine generations, weakening the men precisely at the moment of battle. The unrecognized and mistreated Goddess garners her due by taking away the powers of men. Particularly the power fueling their rage to conquer. She pulls the plug on their battle adrenalin, subduing the urge to kill and the mad drive to control that escalates to the emotional catastrophe zone. Not because of a reduction like emasculation, but because of an enhancement that makes the men suddenly like women. It is impossible for the warrior to fight when he feels the "weakening" of labor. His knees give way and he doubles over in submission to the body. It is the most extraordinary moment of intense world-erasing concentration a human life can know—absurd to call weak on one level—but to the men of Macha the natal takeover destroys the warrior. The demand to submit to the pulse of an inner event (familiar to women) leaves the affairs of the fortress unmanageable and, in time, ensures their defeat.

Unchosen imitation of labor strikes at the belly of masculinity when it is hardened. The Goddess's curse is a cure (as in antidote) for this imperviousness, but it is not uttered in the spirit of peace and light. Fired by vengeance, it comes roaring out to inflict drastic compensation. The king is pulled down from his high horse to twist painfully on the ground in imitation of the mother who bore him. His forehead—in another couvade custom—is "marked like a woman." Like a third eye, he is given to see from his mother's point of view whether he wants to or not. In this bodily travail he remembers her. ("A mother bore every one of you!")

Near the time of birth, mothers are often heard to say that they cannot imagine how anyone could kill another human being. During the Vietnam War this attitude became the Mothers' position: "War is unhealthy for children and other living things." Men tend to say it as well if they have actually been present at the moment of delivery. Studies of male in-

volvement in their partners' childbirth make a dis-
tinction between those present for labor only and
those present for the crowning and birth.[1] It is not
surprising that the latter become (1) more poetic
and (2) less litigious, meaning they are less argumen-
tative and less inclined to sue. The analysis suggests
that the fathers who witnessed the mystery are
touched. Touched perhaps by a mentor like Bacchus,
the bubbly prophetic one who induces wonderment
and models the flow of eloquence.

"Flowing" of feeling is a clue that gender boundaries (especially where they are severely drawn) are
being crossed. Klaus Theweleit's first volume of
*Male Fantasies*, subtitled *Women, Floods, Bodies,
History*, gives a startling and convincing picture of a
massive dam at the emotional core of fascism. He is
working with masculinity gone mad in the minds of
men in the Freikorps—bands of ex-army men serv-
ing the cause of domestic repression after World War
One, progenitors of the Nazis in the Second World
War. Their horrifying, puritanical rigidity defended
against the liquidity of femininity—the amniotic
sea, the riot of life in the uterine spring, the let down
of milk and menses, the secretions of love. All the
abandon they associated with the wild, disorderly
promiscuity of woman they also associated with
Communism. A man must hold himself firm against
the wave, be it of woman, of Communism, whatever the disheveling energy is that would suck him
in. All that is wet and luscious must be dammed up

---

[1] From *The Place of Birth*, pp. 168 and 171. See also Richman's article, "Men's Experiences of Pregnancy and Childbirth," in *The Father
Figure*, ed. L. McKee and M. O'Brien (London: Tavistock, 1982).

and held back by the man of steel who thrives on hatred and self-denial.[1]

Theweleit examines the letters and intimate journals of these men to discover a consistent disavowal of relationship with real women. Their passion is reserved for the Fatherland, for fathers-in-law who have money, for horses, for battle, fellow countrymen, animals. They only refer to women in passing as an occasional exalted vision or in the objectified third person. No personal mother or wife as mother or child is named with either personal appellation or any designation approximating "beloved." Births of children are only perfunctorily mentioned, if at all. In the perversion of their imagination, the blood of childbirth is "unthinkable" and the bloodbaths of murdering women and children are "thinkable."

After wars men want babies in order to become "good," to atone for wartime evils. Having a child is considered a means for reinforcing ties to normal life that have been severed. Men also seek in fatherhood the recognition of maturity outside the structure of the military hierarchy. Birth processes ask ultimate flexibility of those in attendance. Standing at attention does not work in this situation. Attendants have to bend to it, they have to flex to attend. Birth requires a psychological position opposite that of the soldier. To be present, a man has to be capable of being moved. This is what Macha, who knew about horses, battle expectancy, and bloodmesses, decreed when she said that the woman's time of greatest difficulty had to be played out by the armored man.

[1] (Minneapolis: University of Minnesota Press, 1987). See Barbara Ehrenreich's foreword, p. xv.

The way this works in couvade is illustrated by this current dream of a woman who has just given birth. The analyst, to whom she has a father transference, was lying twisted and laboring on the floor in some sort of archaic delivery contraption. As in the "archaic" practice of the man putting on the woman's objects or garments in order to ease her pain, the one in the helper role eases the process (in the sense of moving it along) by being moved. Birth in the consulting room is eased by this capability of the analyst for simulating labor. It's the moment of couvade's necessary slippage. When mastery yields to mystery. The father analyst slips off his chair onto the floor, the king falls off his horse, the warrior lays down his arms. It works because there is an element of consent coursing through the analytical scene, as well as in the practice of couvade. Pain transfers successfully from the wife in labor to the attending husband, near or far, only if he volunteers to take it on. If he tries to escape it, he may be put to bed with the pains anyway (with no relief to the wife) as in the Yorkshire case where a mother found the man who sired her daughter's illegitimate child by going out to locate the first townsman "keeping to his bed" that day. But if he willingly adopts labor, he lessens her pain in proportion to the degree he suffers it.

Weakening the habitual stance of defended manhood by choice seemed ludicrous to most early white male explorers who came upon the living practice of couvade. The men that Dawson quotes probably saw the natives as the heathens from the church hymnal "who, in their blindness, bow down to wood and stone." They called them worse: "block-

heads," "poor fellows," "poor blackies," "laugh-
ing stocks of mankind." Many of their accounts
are so twisted by racist bias that it is hard to extract any detail of what actually happened. Almost
none of the observers recorded what they actually
heard, i.e., the words spoken by someone in the
enactment. In the mid-1700s Captain Cook's voyage
around the world took him to the Society Islands
where he and his men were greeted with a spectac-
ular drama called "The Child Is Coming." Six-
foot, brawny black men enacted a birth—a man
pregnant, a man in labor, and a man child born with
a long wisp of straw attached to his navel. Meanwhile, in what is now called America, the Califor-
nian husband put himself to bed when the child was
coming. He grunted and groaned, "affecting to suffer all the agonies of a woman in labor." He had to
be vegetarian and could not leave the house (in
1759).

Had these early observers been able to listen to
the oral tradition of their grandmothers or to read
classical mythology closely with an eye to what they
were witnessing, they would have found sources for
these seemingly freakish instances of men miming
women.

Shifting contours of male musculature, softening
of the hard edge of difference between the sexes, and
the surrender to the rhythms of the woman all in-
dicate a man's preparation for going somewhere
specific. We cannot know where the native men
thought Captain Cook was going, but if they saw
him as roaming and homeless, a drama about the
mother makes imaginal sense. In Greek mythology
the shift and surrender meant a man was preparing

to descend to the underworld. A man made ready
for this journey at a time in life when he was "at a
loss," when he grieved and roamed, not as a young
boy leaving home, but rather as a man who has lost
his way.

When thigh-born Dionysos goes looking for access to the underworld, he is trying to find a way in
to his mother who died when he was prematurely
lifted into his father's makeshift womb. We know he
is at an entrance when he reaches the edge of desperation corresponding to the edge of a spring-fed
lake flanked by mountains. Here, like the Papuan,
he meets his mentor, or, like Christian at the
slough, he meets Help. Dionysos encounters a figure
called Pathfinder ("Maker-of-Many-Songs-to-the-
Phallus") who will show him the way down only if
he promises complete female surrender.[1] Presumably this was enacted by his sitting on a mortuary
phallus erected on that spot in tribute to the dead.
Dionysos, elsewhere called the Penetrator, had to
yield to penetration in order to find what was lost
beneath his own surface.

A man mid-way finds his mother when he develops a feel for the continuum of birthing. Yielding
to penetration comes before the conception and increase. The yielding means a change in attitude. The
"hard ass," as we say of the one who is tough and
ungiving, is tapped by a Dionysian wand that
loosens. A mindset loosens to permit entry into a
chamber designated "underworld." We could also
call this place he enters "the interior," "the matrix of
inner life," "your natal village." In any case, we are

---

[1] Karl Kerényi, *Dionysos: Archetypal Image of Indestructible Life*
(Princeton: Princeton University Press, 1959), p. 311.

no longer on the surface of a subject once we open it
to psychological penetration. We "go deeper" in
order to "bring out." When a man goes deep enough
into himself, he locates these capacities for conception and containment that belong to mothering.
Darwin stayed here for a while in his fantasies of
male mothering among the species; as with frogs,
for example, he could imagine taking the chaplets of
eggs from the female like a string of meditation
beads and wrapping them around his own thigh.

When the male point of view shifts, a man can be
aware of the heat of his own thighs as an incubating
warmth (rather than as fueling for ejaculation). This
is the proprioceptive data that the poet Charles
Olson urges us into in his description of a body's
awareness as listening to the data-giving depths of
your own tissue. Men's bodies have been sending up
signals of distress. There is currently not enough
cultural room for their mimetic impulse to flower
into full performance. The actual pregnancy-related
symptoms of a husband's backache, nausea, weight
gain, edema, and fatigue—labeled by alert physi-
cians in the 1960s as the "couvade syndrome"—are
part of the greater pathology that threatens the imagination. It is a sickness resulting from the power
of an impacted mystery.

Suffering the mystery to be lived through your
own body can result in a man's being unexpectedly
thrown—as when the pulse of contraction throws
him into his own labor. The taut muscles, the tight-
ening, and the strain to hold make the hand of the
poet tremble as he says, "I drew the woolen shawl
up over my body" (James Moore) to instinctively
take cover under the garment woven by women,

weavers of tissue to bone. His role in creation, as in procreation, expands vastly under the cover of couvade because he can act as a receiver and carrier of the life force rather than solely as progenitor. Thus he gets to have a palatial interior life, labyrinthine levels of meaning to explore, red niches to dig souls out of, and deep enclosures for his own not-yet-born.

Pythagoras the philosopher found himself thrown to the sand by the Night Striding Thunderer at the onset of his initiatory passage.[1] He enacted the re-entry to the mother by lying with a black wreath of wool around his head for a night while facing out toward the dark sea. After the night passed, he made his way down into a cave where he spent "thrice nine days"—precisely the time of a woman's cycle —before he was given to see the "Thunderstone" (the child) on the draped throne (lap of God) looming out of the rocky interior. His transformation occurred under the sign of the thunderstorm that makes all things new. Flowers blossom and youths sprout in the freshly charged air. As with all initiations the aim is renewal through immersion. Boys in Australia who are lowered into rock holes and drawn out by male mothers (men with the vaginal engraving) are similarly reborn. All initiatory wandering is in the mother, through the mother, from mother, to mother. And as Norman O. Brown notes, the transition from matriarchy to patriarchy is always with us and gets us nowhere.[2]

In other words, simple couvade as role reversal gets us nowhere. Men acting as mothers in cultures

[1] *Themis*, pp. 56–59.
[2] *Love's Body* (New York: Vintage Books, 1968), p. 35.

where it was necessary to adhere to a gender-based division of labor are functioning in a ritualized manner that serves to keep gender lines intact. Periodic disturbance of roles around carnival time—or even complete reversals as in the couvade instances where men go to bed to nurse and women go back to the fields—permits an archetypally desired exchange to occur, but the "time out" is followed by a settling back into reliable difference. Couvade consciousness, as we have been attempting it here, wants to blur the boundaries. There are ways of entering and dwelling in the domain of the other. It's not playacting we want, but rather an opening to the play of these images in the psyche.

Intricate customs of couvade that once served to keep men and women in their elaborately circumscribed places provide us with the imaginal details we need to respond to the crisis of "the wandering dead" in the twentieth century. Feminists in the 1970s framed the scenes of desperation in our intimate arrangements resulting from having mothers too largely present and fathers so critically absent. We wander half-alive like "shades" in need of retrieval because we are partially starved. Dorothy Dinnerstein, Adrienne Rich, and Nancy Chodorow esespecially focused on this need. Children need fathers who do what mothers are socially constructed to do. In couvade terms, the fathers need to hatch rather than hunt. And women, who are unhappy in heterosexual relationships because there is no one emotionally and psychologically available to recreate them on a feeling level, need for men to find their own paps. Like the Gaelic saint who had one breast filled with milk and the other filled with honey. Children born to adults unfamiliar with images of the nurturant male are raised to believe the title of the Sicilian folk tale "Anything Can Happen in the World except That Men Become Pregnant."

Reading "The Custom of Couvade" quickens the listener's perception so that we can guess the folk tale goes on to say that the Count did become pregnant and submitted, eventually, to the whole female drama. Stories like "Anything Can Happen," the origin myths, and Dawson's collection of customs lend support to the theory that caretaking behavior is not inherent or "natural to" one sex but rather a human construction with deep psychological, socioeconomic, tradition-bound footings. We are taught that only women will to mother. Yet there is evidence to the contrary if we look to uncover it. Not the least of which is male disorientation and illness resulting from thwarted desire to participate in childbirth. Searching under the symptom of a husband with couvade syndrome, we see that the man who can't bear the smell of certain foods has something in common with the man from Borneo who refrains from skinning the deer or tigercat in his cooking area during pregnancy because he wants to "establish a certain odour" in which his child alone can thrive.

There is an aesthetic of couvade that a man practices when imitating the woman who lives with a tender bloom in her keep. He is aware of scents. His eyes become distinctly sensitized to beauty. His ears attune to soft sound. The Navajo man takes care to protect the unborn child from hearing the screech of a night owl (which could result in the child's having damaged vocal cords).[1] In daylight he is careful to avoid seeing dead cats, horned toads, swollen cows—anything ugly, more dead than alive. He keeps track of his visual mishaps because there are definite ceremonies he can perform if he has seen blood or violence or a dead animal. His endangered child can be healed by singing over it with colors and bits of masks representing that which the father should not have looked upon. Every effort is made to establish an atmosphere of delicacy and sensual comfort.

When such effort fails, the paternal response is to pause to examine his own life: where he's been, what he has seen. Then these details about his deviation from the Beauty Way are relayed to the child. If a baby is born with an enlarged stomach, for example, a father might remember that he saw a bloated fish dead along the shore or in his dream. He can make a small fish figure out of cornmush to place on the hand of the infant as an offering. The act of recollection and the consequential "making something of it" create a healing space. Within it the bond between father and child is acknowledged, given form, and offered up to the inadvertently maligned image of Beauty—by which health is measured. Couvade's aesthetic would designate things "beautiful" according to what infant life requires for its sustenance. Most notably, an atmosphere that is delicate, fragrant, and harmonious.

Dawson's accounts of couvade practices show

[1] Flora L. Bailey, "Some Sex Beliefs and Practices in a Navajo Community," Papers of the Peabody Museum of American Archaeology and Ethnology 40, no. 2 (Cambridge: Harvard University Press, 1950).

HOW THE HUSBAND ASSISTS IN THE BIRTH OF A CHILD

that the man's intention is to sometimes relieve the mother, sometimes to assist the child. A man in a Mexican Huichol yarn painting, called "How the Husband Assists in the Birth of the Child," mirrors both the woman and the child. He lies as the woman does, outstretched. He radiates golden energy on a purple field perhaps cut off from her physically (lying inside the hut while she lies outside on the ground). They are intimately and essentially connected by the life cord tied around his genitals and extending downward toward her open palms, thus displaying an exquisite sensitivity to each other in the birth moment. Below their navels, the tripartite form of the brown child mirrors the dark fruit of the father's sex. As the attendants reach for the emerging child, the chain of life lengthens: the blood blanket around its small form is the same vibrant red as their heart swaths. All of nature is connected in the male and female reach of the event. Even the plants extend toward each other—tendrils toward fruit—resembling the open, root-exposed pose of the birthing parents.

In this painting we are privy to the living pulse of an assistance pattern that Dawson documented around the world. It shows us how the father is born in the moment of the child's emergence: "He who was separate, is no longer." Our reverie about this particular enactment of the male childbed, as with the other instances of broodmale performance, rests on the points of Dawson's compass. As he describes it in his introduction, he has drawn these puzzling customs together into a "convenient compass" for our use. Ours is not to add more horizon points to his instrument (this is the province of anthropology) but to get our bearings from his examples, to linger in the images, to feel their intensity, sense their color, and note their psychological resonance.

The Custom of Couvade

WARREN R. DAWSON

# PREFACE

THE custom of couvade, one of the most curious
ever adopted by man, has for centuries impressed
inquirers by its oddity and puzzled them as to its
interpretation. Much has been written on the subject, and in the bibliography at the end of this
volume are assembled many records of the observation of the custom of couvade—the earliest
dating from the beginning of the Christian era—
and many works that discuss its significance and
attempt to explain it. In Chapters II. to VI. are
grouped, roughly in geographical order, instances
of the occurrence of the custom; in Chapter VII.
its geographical distribution as a whole is considered; and in the final chapter is a summary of
the views put forward by various writers as to the
meaning of the custom, together with some comments thereon. By reserving the comments for the
last chapter, it has not been necessary to encumber
the text with numerous remarks, and consequently
the material is merely arrayed without digression.

This little book is built up very largely of
extracts from the works of actual observers of the
custom, and from those of well-known authorities
who have discussed it. It has been considered better
to state the facts in the various authors' own words
rather than to paraphrase or epitomize them,
except in a few cases where the passages were too

long or too obscure to be presented in their original form. In every case references are given, so that my extracts or summaries can be verified. Amongst the most valuable contributions to the subject are those of the late Sir Edward Tylor, the late Mr. H. Ling Roth, and Sir James Frazer. I have freely made use of all the material brought together by these and other writers, and have supplemented this by references to a number of other publications that have appeared since the works of my predecessors were published, or were overlooked by them. I have been careful in all cases to verify the bibliographical references (and, incidentally, I found many in need of correction), and in all but a few cases have consulted the original works. The bibliography does not claim to be a complete one of its subject, but all the works therein enumerated bear directly upon the custom of couvade or closely related topics; all other works consulted or quoted are referred to in the footnotes.

I cannot claim to have solved the problem of couvade, but at the same time I hope I have succeeded in clearing away some of the valueless debris that has hitherto encumbered the discussion. My object has been to collect into a convenient compass the material for the reconsideration of a puzzling and interesting problem. These materials have been gathered from nearly two hundred different sources, many of them not easy of access. Some further material is considered in the Addenda.

W. R. D.

London, *December* 1928.

# CHAPTER 1

## INTRODUCTION

*N.B.—The numbers in Clarendon Type refer to the Bibliography at the end of this volume.*

THE word *couvade* was first used by Tylor as a technical term in anthropology to designate a series of related customs connected with childbirth (124).[1] These customs require that the father of a child, at or before its birth and for some time after the event, should take to his bed, submit himself to diet and behave generally as though he, and not his wife, were undergoing the rigours of the confinement. In its perfect form, the husband observing the couvade takes to his bed and pretends to be lying-in, sometimes even simulating by groans and contortions the pains of labour, and sometimes even dressing in his wife's clothes. Whilst in bed, he is pampered and fed on dainties, nurses the infant, and receives the felicitations of his relatives and friends.

[1] The word *couvade* is French, and means "brooding" or "hatching". For its etymology, see *The New English Dictionary* ["The Oxford English Dictionary"], vol. ii. p. 1099. Cf. also **1; 35; 124**. It has also been suggested that *couvade* is derived from the Spanish *encovar*, *cueva*, etc., and refers to the covering, or withdrawing, of the husband (**78**, p. 198). This etymology is not generally accepted. Some German ethnologists have termed the custom *Männerkindbett*, whence the English name of "man childbed" is sometimes employed.

Frequently for some time before the birth, and in some instances from the very commencement of his wife's pregnancy, the husband is required to submit to a strict diet and to avoid hard work or the handling of weapons and tools, and to abstain from hunting, smoking and other amusements. In the following chapters will be found numerous instances of these curious procedures, as well as of many degenerate forms of couvade. In the latter, the part played by the husband often amounts to little more than the observance of certain food taboos and some restriction upon his usual occupations. Even in the most complete forms of couvade, the husband's lot is not always a happy one: he is not always the pampered object of his wife's attentions, but often has to submit to starvation for a long period and to ceremonies that involve him in severe physical pain. Many variations of the custom will be found amongst the actual recorded cases collected in the subsequent chapters, but, no matter what precise form the custom may assume, the underlying principle is always evident.

Before passing on to the consideration of the actual cases of couvade in many lands, there are two cases that deserve special consideration, since these are in the nature of religious ceremonies, and as such stand quite apart from the customary form of couvade which is practised only by individual husbands upon the actual birth of a child. It will be convenient to deal with these two instances, from Cyprus and from Ireland respectively, before proceeding further.

Giraud-Teulon tells us that a form of couvade was practised in Cyprus, and says "chez les Cypriens un homme se met au lit et imite les cris et les con-

tortions d'une femme en couches" (39). He quotes
Plutarch's *Theseus* (80) as his authority for this
statement. On referring to Plutarch's text, however, we find that this case is altogether exceptional,
for the rite referred to is clearly part of a religious
ceremony. In this instance the couvade is a pure
fiction, for it is not performed by a husband upon
the birth of a child as is the case in all normal cou-
vades throughout the world.

Plutarch relates that Theseus, whose ship was
driven upon the coast of Cyprus during a storm,
there landed Ariadne, who was then on the eve of
confinement. Returning to attend to the anchorage
of his vessel, the tempest immediately carried the
ship out to sea, and Theseus was thus involuntarily
parted from Ariadne. Meanwhile Ariadne, who
was received kindly by the Cyprian women, gave
birth to her child, but died at its delivery. Theseus,
returning soon after, was distracted with grief, and
on leaving the island "he left a sum of money among
the inhabitants, ordering them to make sacrifice to
Ariadne, and caused two little images to be made;
the one of silver, the other of bronze. Moreover, on
the second day of the month Gorpiaeus [Septem-
ber], which is sacred to Ariadne, they have this
ceremony among their sacrifices: to have a youth
lie down and by his voice and gestures simulate the
pains of a woman in travail" (80).[1]

The idea of couvade, namely, a man simulating

---

[1] ἐπελθόντα δὲ τὸν Θησέα καὶ περίλυπον γενόμενον τοῖς μὲν
ἐγχωρίοις ἀπολιπεῖν χρήματα, συντάξαντα θύειν τῇ Ἀριάδνῃ, δύο
δὲ μικροὺς ἀνδριαντίσκους ἱδρύσασθαι, τὸν μὲν ἀργυροῦν, τὸν δὲ
χαλκοῦν. ἐν δὲ τῇ θυσίᾳ τοῦ Γορπιαίου μηνὸς ἱσταμένου δευτέρᾳ
κατακλινόμενόν τινα τῶν νεανίσκων φθέγγεσθαι καὶ ποιεῖν ἅπερ
ὠδίνουσαι γυναῖκες.

the pains of childbirth, clearly underlies this curious ceremony instituted by Theseus in commemoration of the fatal labour of Ariadne.

The other exceptional case is a Celtic legend from Ireland, and this has come down to us in two manuscripts of the twelfth and fifteenth centuries respectively. A translation, with a philological commentary, was published many years ago, first by Windisch (137) and later by H. D'Arbois de Jubanville (51), from which the story may be summarized as follows:

There was a certain rich Ulster farmer named Crunniuc, whose wife died. After some time a mysterious woman entered the house, and immediately made herself fully at home, tending the children, ordering the household and acting generally as if she had ever belonged to the family. In course of time she conceived by Crunniuc, and the date of her expected delivery coincided with the great festival called Oenach. Owing to her condition, she was unable to attend the fête, but her husband set off, receiving from his wife a parting injunction to say nothing imprudent. In the course of the festival there was a horse-race, and it was won by the king's horses. "Could anything be swifter than these horses?" said the bystanders. "My wife can run faster," said Crunniuc. This imprudent utterance, made in entire disregard of his wife's warning, was overheard by the king, who took it as an insult, and gave orders for the arrest of Crunniuc. The king further ordered that the wife should be brought forthwith to run a race with his horses.

The king's messengers accordingly set out to fetch the wife of Crunniuc. His wife declared that

Crunniuc was wrong in his statement, but that in any case her condition prevented her compliance with the king's order, and she begged passionately for delay. The king's command, however, had to be obeyed, and the hapless woman was dragged off to the course. Arrived there, she made a further fervent appeal, for she already felt the pains of labour. The exasperated king ordered Crunniuc to be beheaded. Yet again the woman begged for delay until her delivery should be accomplished, but the relentless king still refused. The woman thereupon uttered a solemn declaration that for the wrong done to her the king should suffer a greater. "What is your name?" inquired the king. "I am called Macha," she replied, "the daughter of the Stranger [Sainred] Son of the Ocean [Imbath]; the place of this festival shall ever bear my name and that of that which is within my womb. Make ready the horses!"

The race began, and when the king's horses reached the winning-post, Macha had already arrived. There and then, beneath the very horses' heads, she gave birth to twins, a boy and a girl; and the place was thenceforth known as the "Twins of Macha" [Emain Macha], and was long the capital of Ulster. At the moment of her delivery, Macha uttered a loud cry. All the men who heard it were struck with a kind of enchantment. They were doomed to suffer once in their life the pains of childbirth for five days and four nights or for four days and five nights. This was called "The *Nine-night Week* of the Ulates".[1] During this period the men had no more strength than a woman in

[1] Concerning this week, cf. **85**, pp. 360, 365.

travail, and this strange affliction passed from
father to son for nine generations. From this curse
only the hero Cuchulainn was exempted. When the
epic queen Medb invaded the kingdom of the
Ulates [Ulster], and began the war which is the
subject of the principal Irish epics, all the warriors
of Ulster were afflicted with their predicted curse,
and, with the single exception of Cuchulainn, were
unable to fight.

This remarkable story is evidently of mytho-
logical origin. The enforced couvade of the men
was the vengeance of the outraged goddess for the
wrongs done to her. It has a curious parallel in the
story related by Herodotus of the vengeance of the
injured deity upon the Scythians, who had pillaged
her temple in the Syrian city of Askalon. "The
goddess inflicted on the Scythians who robbed her
temple at Askalon, and on all their posterity, a
female disease; so that the Scythians confess that
they are afflicted with it on that account, and those
who visit Scythia may behold the state of those
whom the Scythians call Enarees." [1]

We do not know the nature of the disease that
the goddess inflicted upon those who had wronged
her, but the Scythian and Irish stories are exact
parallels in that an affliction peculiar to women was
in both cases transferred to men. We shall have
occasion to refer in a later chapter to these remarkable legends.

[1] Herodotus, i. 105 τοῖσι δὲ τῶν Σκυθέων συλήσασι τὸ ἱρὸν
τὸ ἐν Ἀσκάλωνι καὶ τοῖσι τούτων αἰεὶ ἐκγόνοισι ἐνέσκηψε ὁ θεὸς
θήλεαν νοῦσον. ὥστε ἅμα λέγουσί τε οἱ Σκύθαι διὰ τοῦτό σφεας
νοσέειν, καὶ ὁρᾶν παρ' ἑωυτοῖσι τοὺς ἀπικνεομένους ἐς τὴν Σκυθικὴν
χώρην ὡς διακέαται, τοὺς καλέουσι ἐνάρεας οἱ Σκύθαι.

We may also note some further customs which may properly be considered in connection with couvade. Hesychius and other writers refer to an ancient Athenian custom called Amphidromia, in which a new-born child is carried round the domestic hearth. M. Salomon Reinach, in an interesting study of this custom (84), points out that the child was not carried round by the mother, nor by any other woman (as often erroneously stated), but was borne by a *man*, a naked man, who seized the child and ran round the hearth. He explains the significance both of the running and the nakedness of the runner, and brings evidence to show that the object of the rite was to make the child active and swift of foot, and quotes some striking modern survivals of the custom. The performance of this act by the father (rather than the mother) for the benefit of the child brings the rite, in the opinion of M. Reinach, into the same category as other acts of sympathetic magic performed by a father for the welfare of his child, of which he considers couvade to be a conspicuous example.

The rearing of infants by men, a custom which, according to Diodorus Siculus, was observed by the Amazons of Western Libya, may possibly be connected with couvade. There were two legendary races of Amazons: those of Pontus, near the borders of the Black Sea,[1] and those of Libya.[2] In both these tribes the women exclusively managed all the affairs of government, and the army was composed solely of female soldiers. To the men were relegated all menial duties and all household cares,

[1] Herodotus, iv. 110-117; Diodorus Siculus, ii. 44.
[2] Diodorus Siculus, iii. 53.

together with the rearing of children. In the words of Diodorus, "when the Amazons bear children, the male infants are immediately handed over to the men, who rear them on milk or upon cooked foods, according to the age of the children. As to the female infants, as soon as they are born, their breasts are burnt, so that they do not grow with the other parts of their bodies, and that the development of the breasts may not be an obstacle to military exercises." According to other accounts, the right breast only was amputated in order that it might not impede the use of the bow. This superiority of women and consequent subordination of men—the gynecocracy—is held by some writers to be related to couvade (*e.g.* **13**); but whether there be any relationship or not, both are interesting examples of the inversion of the usual functions of the sexes, or of the simulating by the one the status of the other.

A Basque legend concerning the origin of couvade is related in the Addenda (see p. 139).

# CHAPTER II

## THE COUVADE IN EUROPE

In the previous chapter we have called attention to a curious custom formerly practised in Cyprus, which, if not true couvade, is closely related to it. The next instance to be noticed is that of Corsica, where, according to Diodorus Siculus, the custom was practised in ancient times. Writing of the Corsicans in the first century A.D., Diodorus informs us that "one of the most curious features of their customs is that which they observe at the birth of their children. When a woman becomes a mother she pays no heed to the period of lying-in; but her husband, as though he were an invalid, takes to his bed and is waited upon during the period of accouchement with as much attention as if he were really suffering bodily pain" (**30**).[1]

A couvade lasting eight days is, or lately was, observed in the Balearic Islands (**78**, p. 198; **6**, p. 778).

As regards Spain, the earliest record of couvade in the Iberian Peninsula is that of Strabo, who

---

[1] παραδοξότατον δ' ἐστὶ τὸ παρ' αὐτοῖς γινόμενον κατὰ τὰς τῶν τέκνων γενέσεις· ὅταν γὰρ ἡ γυνὴ τέκνῃ, ταύτης μὲν οὐδεμία γίνεται περὶ τὴν λοχείαν ἐπιμέλεια, ὁ δ' ἀνὴρ αὐτῆς ἀναπεσὼν ὡς νοσῶν λοχεύεται τακτὰς ἡμέρας, ὡς τοῦ σώματος αὐτῷ κακοπαθοῦντος.

says: "These [pursuits] are common to both sides among the Celtic races in Thrace and Scythia— even manliness is common to men and women. The women till the land, and when they have given birth to children, they put their husbands to bed in their own stead and nurse them" (113).[1]

This account appears to be quite unequivocal, but some modern writers believe that Strabo's statement is open to doubt as to whether couvade is actually referred to (*e.g.* Dr. Murray, 1, p. 459). In view of the abundant testimony—both ancient and modern—that exists as to the custom of couvade elsewhere, there seems to be no good reason for doubting it. Certain writers affirm that the custom has survived amongst the Basques in modern times: such was the opinion of Quatrefages (83) and of Michel (69). Laborde says "les femmes Cantabres portaient les fardeaux les plus lourds; elles culti- vaient les champagnes, labouraient les champs et ne négligeaient aucune espèce de travaux; elles se levaient aussitôt après être accouchies et servaient leurs maris, qui se mettaient au lit à leur place, usage qui fut aussi commun aux habitants de la Navarre, et dont il est impossible de rendre raison" (58).

Zamacola, writing at the beginning of the nine- teenth century, refers to Strabo's account of the ancient Cantabri and says that the modern Basques have the same manners and customs. After men- tioning several points of resemblance, this author

---

[1] κοινὰ δὲ καὶ ταῦτα πρὸς τὰ Κελτικὰ ἔθνη καὶ τὰ Θράκια καὶ Σκυθικά, κοινὰ δὲ καὶ ‹ τὰ πρὸς ἀνδρείαν τήν τε τῶν ἀνδρῶν καὶ τὴν τῶν γυναικῶν. γεωργοῦσι αὗται, τεκοῦσαί τε διακονοῦσι τοῖς ἀνδράσιν, ἐκείνους ἀνθ᾽ ἑαυτῶν κατακλίνασαι.

writes: "And finally [Strabo says] that these women, as soon as they had borne a child, got up from the bed, while the husband lay down in it with the baby, just as was done a short time ago in many parts of Cantabria, because it was a natural duty and a custom amongst the Basques that the first sweat or shelter that the child received should be that of his father to identify him with the humours and spirit of his parents" (141, translated from the Spanish).

Ripley, whilst denying the statement that couvade is practised in Spain at the present day, admits that "there is no likelier spot for it to have survived in Europe than here in the Pyrenees; but it must be confessed that no direct proof of its existence can be found to-day, guide-books to the contrary notwithstanding" (86). A more recent writer has given good grounds for the opinion that couvade is not now, nor has lately been, practised by the Basques, but that the custom or tradition of it survives in other parts of northern Spain, as in the Balearic Islands (6). The general result of the investigation seems to point to the fact that couvade in Spain has not survived to the present day (130), but there seems to be no good reason for doubting either Strabo's statement or the continuance of couvade long after Strabo's time. The statements of such writers as Brissaud (19) are of a purely negative character. This writer, with apparent disregard of the literature of the subject, discusses the alleged statements of a mayor and of a schoolmaster who stated that they had known instances of the custom. He comes to the conclusion that such stories are deliberate attempts at "mysti-

fication", and that there never was couvade amongst
either the Basques or Béarnais; and further, that the
reports of such a custom are modern inventions,
and that the Basques attribute couvade to the
Béarnais and vice versa.

There is too much evidence, both direct and
indirect, that such an "explanation" fails to account
for (see below, p. 140).

We have already seen that Laborde states that
at the commencement of the nineteenth century
couvade was common amongst the inhabitants of
Navarre (58, 59), and in this connection the medi-
eval tradition preserved in the story of Aucassin
and Nicolette is interesting. "Legrand d'Aussy
mentions that in an old French fabliau the king
of Torelore is 'au lit et en couche' when Aucassin
arrives and takes a stick to him, and makes him
promise to abolish the custom in his realm. And
the same author goes on to say that the practice is
still said to exist in some cantons of Bearn, where it
is called *faire la couvade*" (124, pp. 295-296, quoting Legrand d'Aussy, *Fabliaux du XII<sup>e</sup> et XIII<sup>e</sup>
siècles*, 3rd ed., Paris, 1829).

Mention has just been made of the province of
Béarn, on the French side of the Pyrenees. In
France the tradition of couvade has survived in the
old saying, "Il se met au lit quand sa femme est
en couche" (78, p. 197), and in the custom of
placing the husband's garments upon the wife at
the moment of delivery in order to transfer the
pains of childbirth from the latter to the former.
A seventeenth century writer refers thus to the
custom: "Quand une femme est en mal d'enfant
luy faire mettre le haut-de-chausse de son mari,

afin qu'elle accouche sans douleur" (117). Similar
customs have been recorded from Germany (138).[1]

M. Salomon Reinach records a curious ceremony
that was observed about 1880 in a coastal village
near Coutances (Manche), in the north of France.
An infant a few months old had died, and, whilst
waiting for the body to be placed in a little coffin
immediately before its removal to the cemetery,
the child's mother, *and father*, retired to bed and,
reclining there, received the condolences of each
of the mourners invited to the funeral, who came
one by one to the bedside (84, p. 688, note 1).

Whilst making no attempt to explain this
singular custom, it is worthy of being placed
amongst the French survivals of the couvade.

In the British Isles the tradition of couvade
survives in the beliefs still current that the pregnancy or confinement of a woman affects her husband, and that the former is relieved from pain in
proportion as the latter suffers it (15; 33). Such
beliefs have been recorded in recent years from
Oxfordshire, Cheshire, Yorkshire and elsewhere
(2; 15); and similar ideas have degenerated into
"married man's toothache", of which many instances could be given. In the north-east of Scotland a belief still lingers that if the husband is the
first to rise on the morning after his marriage, he
will bear all the pains of childbirth when his wife's
time arrives (91). We have, however, more definite
evidence of couvade than these shadowy traditions.
It was believed in Scotland, for instance, in the
eighteenth century, and probably later, that the

[1] Other German customs which are akin to, or perhaps derived
from, couvade are noted by Hartland (45, pp. 410-411).

nurse could voluntarily transfer the pains of child-birth from the mother to the father. This intro-duces a new element, namely, witchcraft, but the couvade tradition is clear. Thomas Pennant, writ-ing of his visit to Langholm, Dumfriesshire, in 1772, relates that "the midwives had the power of transferring part of the primeval curse bestowed upon our first great mother from the good wife to her husband. I saw the reputed offspring of such a labour, who kindly came into the world without giving her mother the least uneasiness, while the poor husband was roaring with agony and in un-couth and unnatural pains" (76). A similar practice has been recorded from Ireland, where it was believed that the pains of maternity could be trans-ferred from mother to father by the nurse, who made magical use of the man's garments taken from him and laid on the mother. "It is asserted by some that the husband's consent must first be obtained, but the general opinion is that he feels all the pain, and even cries out with agony, without being aware of the cause" (71; similar cases, 41).

There is an old Irish saying that preserves the couvade tradition: "You'll soon have to go to bed with the old woman and be nursed as they did years ago" (33; 78, p. 196). Mr. Donald A. Mac-kenzie informs me that there is an old Highland saying that is still occasionally heard: *Chuir i piantan air an duine*, "put she the pains on the man".

Finally, we may quote the following curious case that appeared in the press in 1884: "We heard lately, from a source that is above suspicion, of the survival in a certain district of Yorkshire of a practice bearing no little resemblance to the *couvade*. When an illegitimate child is born, it is a point of honour with the girl not to reveal the father; but the mother of the girl forthwith goes out to look for him, and the first man she finds keeping his bed is he" (2; also quoted in the *Folk Lore Journal*, vol. ii., 1884, p. 121).

Some further traces of the couvade and of analogous customs in Europe are noted in the Addenda (see below, p. 141).

# CHAPTER III

## THE COUVADE IN AFRICA

DEFINITE instances of the couvade are extremely rare in Africa. There is no trace whatever of the custom in the records of ancient Egypt, and no tradition of it amongst the modern Egyptians. Elsewhere in Africa there are some instances of the idea underlying the custom, *i.e.* the participation by the husband in the risks of the pregnancy of his wife by the imposition on him of certain restrictions. Thus, amongst the Bagesu, a people inhabiting the district of Mount Elgon, north-east of Lake Victoria, a modified form of couvade exists. When a Bagesu woman is pregnant, "her husband has to refrain from climbing any trees or high rocks or on to house-tops, and when walking down a hill he had to go carefully, for, should he slip and fall, his wife might have a miscarriage"(92).

It appears, too, that couvade is practised in the region of the White Nile, Southern Soudan, and also amongst the Dinkas. A correspondent informed Roth that "in the Shuli district the women are held in high esteem. They are looked up to by the men, and counsel is taken of them in most of the affairs of life. In this district, to the best of my belief, couvade really exists, because for some days

before and after a child's birth, the father remains
in or near the hut, refrains from certain kinds of
meat (what, I do not know), and generally takes
care of himself, that the infant may not be harmed.
Again, amongst the Dinkas a somewhat similar
custom obtains. For two or three days after the
birth of a child the father remains in the hut, pays
great attention to it, and nurses it" (**94**, p. 216).

The couvade motive seems to underlie the action
of the natives at Goumbi (Nigeria), related by Du
Chaillu and quoted by Roth (**94**, p. 236). When the
famous traveller brought a female gorilla into camp,
"while she was alive, no woman who was enceinte,
*nor the husband of such woman*, dared approach her
cage. They believe firmly that should the husband
of a woman with child, or the woman herself, see a
gorilla, even a dead one, she would give birth to a
gorilla and not to a man child. This superstition I
have noticed among other tribes too, and only in
the case of the gorilla" (**21**, p. 262). On another
occasion, when the body of a dead gorilla was
brought into the village, three women who were
pregnant hastened from the village *with their
husbands*, and nothing could induce them to return
until the skin of the beast had been dried and put
away, as they were firmly convinced that if even
their husbands saw the animal, the wives would
bear gorillas instead of children (**21**, p. 305).

The missionary Zucchelli found a form of couvade in the eighteenth century amongst a Bantu
people at Kasanje (Congo). Here the husband went
to bed for several days and was tended by his wife
(**142; 143**). Roth doubts the authenticity of this
statement (**94**, p. 216). In the same region of Africa,

however, we have a well-attested modern instance of the occurrence of couvade. The following episode is related of the Bushongo, a tribe living among the Bantu races of the Congo Basin. They are believed to have migrated southwards from the edge of the Sahara, near Lake Tchad, and are related to the Azande:

" From behind a wall a pretty girl looked maliciously at Miko-Mikope, a very handsome young man, who sat in front of his house smoking and tried hard to look unconcerned. It was no good, everyone knew, and the pretty girl knew, that he was as good as a prisoner; his wife was expecting a baby, and, in accordance with the custom of the country, had cut his belt; if he rose, his clothes would fall off, and—oh, horror! at any moment he might be called, not to the bed of his wife, but to go to bed himself and be nursed till the trouble was over" (122).

Possible survivals of the couvade amongst the Boloki of the Congo and in Madagascar are recorded in the Addenda (see below, p. 142).

The Nandi of East Africa have a custom that may possibly be akin to couvade, for a man whose wife is suckling a baby is not allowed to touch the threshold of his dwelling, nor anything within it, except his own bed.[1]

[1] J. G. Frazer, *Folk-Lore in the Old Testament*, vol. iii. (London, 1919), p. 6.

# CHAPTER IV

## THE COUVADE IN ASIA

Two ancient writers, Apollonius Rhodius and
Valerius Flaccus, have recorded the couvade
custom amongst a people called the Tibareni of
Pontus, which is situated to the north-east of
Asia Minor, south of the Black Sea. Apollonius
Rhodius relates that after leaving the mountains
of the Genetaean Zeus, the voyagers reach the
land of the Tibareni; "there, when the women bear
children to their men, the latter take to their beds
and groan with their heads tied up, while the women
pamper them with tasty food and prepare for them
the baths proper to childbirth" (5).[1] The same
people are referred to by Valerius Flaccus, who
says: "Thence they pass the mountain of the Genetaean Jupiter, and put behind them the green
lakes of the Tibarenians, where [the woman]
swaddles her child in the folds of her head-cloth,
and after childbirth nurses her man" (128).[2]

[1] τοὺς δὲ μέτ' αὐτίκ' ἔπειτα Γενηταίου Διὸς ἄκρην
γνάμψαντες σώοντο παρὲξ Τιβαρηνίδα γαῖαν.
ἔνθ' ἐπεὶ ἄρ κε τέκωνται ὑπ' ἀνδράσι τέκνα γυναῖκες,
αὐτοὶ μὲν στενάχουσιν ἐνὶ λεχέεσσι πεσόντες,
κράατα δησάμενοι· ταὶ δ' εὖ κομέουσιν ἐδωδῇ
ἀνέρας, ἠδὲ λοετρὰ λεχώια τοῖσι πένονται.

[2] Inde Genetaei rupem Iovis, hinc Tibarenum
dant virides post terga lacus, ubi deside mitra
feta ligat, partuque virum fovet ipsa soluto.

Couvade has been recorded from many localities
in India. The earliest reference to the custom is
contained in the writings of Alberuni (*c.* 1300 A.D.),
who, speaking of the Hindus, says: "When a child
is born, people show particular attention to the
man, not to the woman" (3). In Southern India
there is a proverb, "'Tis like a Korovan eating asafoetida when his wife lies-in", and this refers to the
couvade custom amongst the low-caste Madras race
of Korovans. "Whereas native women generally
eat asafoetida as a strengthening medicine after
childbirth, it is the husband who eats it to fortify
himself on the occasion. This, in fact, is a variety
of the world-wide custom of 'couvade', where at
childbirth the husband undergoes medical treatment, in many cases being put to bed for days. It
appears that the Korovans are among the races
practising this quaint custom, and that their more
civilized Tamil neighbours, struck by its oddity,
but unconscious of its now forgotten meaning,
have taken it up as a proverb" (125).

At Gujarat a goddess is worshipped whose
power is extended for the benefit of women after
childbirth. "Among a very low-caste set of basket-
makers (called Pomlā) it is the usual practice of a
wife to go about her work immediately after
delivery, as if nothing had happened. The presid-
ing Mātā of the tribe is supposed to transfer her
weakness to her husband, who takes to his bed
and has to be supported with good nourishing
food" (136).

Among the Erekulas or Yerukalas in Southern
India, "directly the woman feels the birth-pangs
she informs her husband, who immediately takes

some of her clothes, puts them on, places on his forehead the mark which the women usually place on theirs, retires into a dark room, where there is only a very dim lamp, and lies down on the bed, covering himself up with a long cloth. When the child is born, it is washed and placed on the cot beside the father, asafoetida, jaggery and other articles are then given, not to the mother, but to the father. During the days of ceremonial uncleanliness, the man is treated as the Hindus treat their women on such occasions. He is not allowed to leave his bed, but has everything needful brought to him" (20).

The following extracts contain many interesting particulars:

"Among the Koravars or basket-makers of Malabar, as soon as the pains of delivery come upon a pregnant woman, she is taken to an outlying shed, and left alone to live or die as the event may turn out. No help is given to her for twenty-eight days. Even medicines are thrown to her from a distance; and the only assistance rendered is to place a jar of warm water close by her just before the child is born. Pollution from birth is held to be worse than that from death. At the end of the twenty-eight days the hut in which she was confined is burnt down. The father, too, is polluted for fourteen days, and at the end of that time he is purified, not like other castes by the barber, but by holy water obtained from the Brāhmans at temples or elsewhere.

"Among various other classes it is customary for the husband to remove the pollution caused by his wife's confinement by means of ceremonial ablution.

"To Mr. G. Krishna Rao, Superintendent of Police in the Shimoga district of Mysore, I am indebted for the following note on the couvade as practised among the Koramas:

" 'Mr. Rice, in the *Mysore Gazette*, says that among the Koravars it is said that, when a woman is confined, her husband takes medicine for her. At the instance of the British Resident, I made inquiries, and learned that the Kukke (basket-making) Koramas, lying at Gopola Village, near Shimoga, had this custom among them. The husband learns from his wife the probable time of her confinement, and keeps at home awaiting the delivery. As soon as she is confined, he goes to bed for three days, and takes medicine consisting of chicken and mutton broth spiced with ginger, pepper, onions, garlic, etc. He drinks arrack, and eats as good food as he can afford, while his wife is given boiled rice with a very small quantity of salt, for fear that a larger quantity may induce thirst. There is generally a Koramar midwife to help the wife, and the husband does nothing but eat, drink and sleep. The clothes of the husband, the wife and the midwife are given to a washer-woman to be washed on the fourth day, and the persons themselves have a wash. After this purifi-cation, the family gives a dinner to the caste-people, which finishes the ceremonial connected with child-birth. One of the men examined by me, who was more intelligent than the rest, explained that the man's life was more valuable than that of the woman, and that the husband, being a more import-ant factor in the birth of the child than the wife, deserves to be better looked after.'

"The following legend is current among the Koramas to explain the practice of couvade among them. One day a donkey belonging to a Korama camp pitched outside a village, wandered into a Brāhman's field, and did considerable damage to the crop. The Brāhman was naturally angry, and ordered his coolies to pull down the hut of the owner of the donkey. The Korama, putting himself at the feet of the Brāhman, for want of a better excuse, said that he was not aware of what his animal was doing, for at the time he was taking medicine for his wife and could not look after it. It is suggested in the Mysore Census Report, 1901, that the practice of the couvade has either long ceased to exist, or is a mere myth based upon a proverb evolved out of a Brāhman's gullibity in accepting the plea that a Korama was eating medicine because his wife was in childbed as a conclusive proof of an alibi on his behalf.

"It is noted by the Rev. S. Mateer (*Journ. Royal Asiatic Soc.* xvi.) that after the confinement of a Paraiyan woman in Travancore, the husband is starved for seven days, eating no cooked rice or other food, only roots and fruits; and drinking only arrack or toddy [171].

"Possibly, as suggested by Reclus, the following Toda custom . . . is a survival of the couvade: After the child is born, the mother is removed to a shed, which has been erected in some sequestered spot, in anticipation of the approaching event. There she remains until the next new moon, and for a month after her return home she appears to have the house to herself, her husband remaining indebted to friends for shelter meanwhile.

"The Nayādis of the Cochin State erect a special small hut to which the woman retires when taken in labour. She is attended to by various female relations, and her husband all the while goes on shampooing his own abdomen, and praying to the mountain gods for the safe delivery of his wife. As soon as the child is born, he offers thanks to them for 'having got the child out' " (120).

The couvade custom does not appear to be confined to the lower castes in India. "[The couvade] is usual among natives of the higher castes about Madras, Seringapatam and on the Malabar coast. It is stated that a man, at the birth of his first son or daughter by the chief wife, or for any son afterwards, will retire to bed for a lunar month, living principally on a rice diet, abstaining from exciting food and from smoking; at the end of the month he bathes, puts on a fresh dress and gives his friends a feast" (124, 2nd ed. p. 301).

The custom of couvade has been recorded from various parts of Northern India. Thus amongst the Miri tribe of the Brahmaputra valley "the father is represented as a second mother, and goes through the fiction of a mock-birth, the so-called *couvade*. He lies in bed for forty days after the birth of his child; and during this period he is fed as an invalid" (131).

In Assam couvade is practised by various tribes (42). "Among the Tangkhuls the husband may not go out of the village or do any work after the birth of a child for six days if the child be a boy, or for five days when the child is a girl" (46).

The following birth customs of the Hindus in Northern India are akin to couvade, in that the

father plays the prominent rôle: "Among those
castes which follow Brahminical rules, after the
child is born, the first birth rite is performed. The
father bathes, offers prayers 'to the god Ganesa,
patron of good-luck and remover of obstacles, im-
ploring him that the child may be good, strong and
wise; that, if she has become specially impure by
violating any of the prescribed rules of conduct or
food, the mother's sin may be forgiven, and that
its consequences may not be visited upon the baby.
He then invokes the sainted ancestors of his family,
of the nine planets which preside over domestic
rites. With a golden skewer or the third finger of
his right hand he smears the tongue of the child
with a mixture of butter and honey, while a prayer
is recited asking that the child may be endowed
with all material blessings. The father then takes
the child in his arms, and, touching each member of
its body while reciting the suitable formula, prays
that they (sic) may be endowed with strength.
Finally, the father is purified by asperging him
with holy water sprinkled from a brush made of
sacred grass. The husband thus joins in the taboo
which surrounds his wife, a belief which is probably
at the root of the curious custom of the couvade"
(26).

Similar purification ceremonies are performed
by the father in Central India. "This habit of the
husband taking a purifying dose after his wife has
borne a child is very common among many of the
forest tribes of Central India. The father is purified
in a different way by the Deshasht Brāhmans of
Bombay, who insist, when a birth occurs in the
family, on the father jumping into a well with all

his clothes on; after which he is allowed to pour drops of honey and butter into the child's mouth, as a sign that it is admitted into the caste" (25).

Writing on the Sonjhara caste of the Central Provinces, Russell states: "In Bilāspur the Sonjharas observe the custom of the couvade, and for six days after the birth of a child, the husband lies prone in his house, while the wife gets up and goes to work, coming home to give suck to the child when necessary. The man takes no food for three days, and on the fourth is given ginger and raw sugar, thus undergoing the ordinary treatment of a woman after childbirth. This is supposed by them to be a sort of compensation for the labours sustained by the woman in bearing the child". The custom is now dying out (96).

The Venetian traveller Marco Polo describes the custom in Zardandau, in Chinese Turkestan: "And when one of their wives has been delivered of a child, the infant is washed and swathed, and the woman gets up and goes about her household duties, whilst the husband takes to bed with the child by his side, and so keeps his bed for forty days; and all the kith and kin come to visit him and keep up a great festivity. They do this because, they say, the woman has had a hard bout of it, and 'tis but fair that the man should have his share of the suffering" (140, p. 52).

The Langzi, the aborigines of the department of Weihing, observe the couvade for forty days (as do also, as we have seen, the Miris of Assam). It was probably Marco Polo's story that gave rise to Butler's allusion in *Hudibras* (iii. Canto i, 70):

For though Chineses go to bed
And lie-in, in their ladies' stead.

It appears, however, that the real Chinese do not practise couvade, and the above-named instances gave a false impression (32).[1] The custom, however, was formerly observed by the Ainu of Japan. Batchelor records that "a curious custom used to exist amongst this people. As soon as the child was born, the father had to consider himself very ill, and had, therefore, to stay at home, wrapped by the fire. But the wife, poor creature! had to stir about as much and as quickly as possible. The idea seems to have been that life was passing from the father into his child" (11).

The most northerly locality in Asia in which any trace of the couvade can be found is Kamchatka, where the husband's operations are restricted before the birth of a child. He is not allowed to do heavy or dangerous work, such as bending sledge-staves across his knee, as such actions would harm his wife (124, p. 292). In his account of Kamchatka, Steller relates the following episode: "It happened in my time that a woman as a rare case had a child which was born with a breech-presentation, and she had to endure the pains of labour for three days. The Shamans said that the man was responsible for it, as, at the time the child was born, he was making a sledge, and necessarily bent the staves into their curved shape across his knee, from which one can see the absurd fancies of the inhabitants" (112, translated).

[1] On this point, see below, p. 143.

# CHAPTER V

## THE COUVADE IN THE ISLANDS [1]

RETURNING now to the southern part of the Asiatic continent, we can trace the custom through the long series of islands in the Indian Ocean, and through Indonesia and Melanesia.

Beginning nearest to the Indian coast, we find couvade practised in the Nicobar group, concerning which we have, fortunately, very full information. The custom was briefly alluded to in a paper on the Nicobarese, published by E. H. Man in 1889, who said: "[Couvade] is practised by all the communities at the Nicobars, including the inland tribe of Great Nicobar; it is by them regarded as a custom of remote antiquity, and is called *otô* in the dialect of the Central Group" (**66**).

A much fuller statement by the same author was quoted by Roth a few years later, and as this narrative contains so much of interest, I make no apology for quoting it in full:

"Although never, I believe, mentioned or even known to previous writers, the singular custom called 'couvade' or paternal lying-in is among the institutions of the Nicobarese: it is called *falngendre*,

[1] A small part of the mainland, the southern extremity of the Malay Peninsula, is included in this chapter.

and is practised at Car Nicobar, as also in the southern islands of the group; the period extends over some two weeks for a first child, during which time the man may not work nor cook, but lies up like an invalid, while he and his wife are fed by their relatives. If a man marries a second wife after having had children by the former marriage, the couvade, upon his again becoming a father, is curtailed to a couple of days.

"Among the Nicobarese couvade is likened to the sitting of a hatching hen. At Nancoury the husband must remain as an invalid for about five days, during which he may not work, nor chew betel, nor bathe, and he has his food cooked for him and brought to him. He may feed his wife with what is thus cooked and brought to him. After this, and until his wife is able to resume her ordinary duties, he must still refrain from leaving the village or from joining in any entertainments, and he can only perform work of a light nature, but may eat what food he likes.

"A day or more before the confinement, in order to ensure an easy labour, the lashings of the husband's and her own property, e.g. canoes, spears, waterpots, and even of the hut, etc., are cut, and they are renewed soon after the birth of the child.

"The food forbidden to a woman from the time of her confinement till she resumes her duties a month or so later are fish (including turtles and crabs), fowl and cocoanut. Her drink consists of hot water, and her food of vegetables, fruit, rice, pandanus and pork.

"At Car Nicobar it is much the same, only there the husband remains idle and has his food cooked for him for about one month. He may bathe two days after the birth of his child.

"In some cases husbands consider it advisable to observe greater precautions by commencing to do little or no work a few months before their wife's expected confinement, more especially abstaining from any such work as felling trees and digging holes for hut posts.

"The belief is that if the father failed to observe the custom of couvade the child would be liable to fits; and were the infant to ail or die under such circumstances, it would certainly be attributed to the father's failure to observe the practice.

"Similar observances are found throughout the group. The Nicobarese are not matriarchal. The mother looks after the child, assisted by her female friends. Some slight modifications occur in the case of a man's first child. The observance is less strict in the case of a man who has a child by a second wife, if he has had children by his late wife" (**94**, pp. 214-216).

To this most interesting account of couvade in the Nicobars, we can add another, that of Mr. George Whitehead, a recent writer (**134**):

"During the latter part at least, say two months, of the wife's pregnancy both parents must abstain from certain kinds of food and from certain actions, as also for some time after birth. The restrictions are binding on the father as much as on the mother, and though the couvade does not prevail in its fullness in Car Nicobar, there are traces of it in other matters than in restrictions about food. When the prospective mother goes down to *el-panam* (the beach where the birth and dead houses,

etc. are) her husband goes along with her; though
the less sophisticated Car Nicobarese say that this
is not due to the father's birth-pains, but in order
that he may be ready, at all times, to wait on his
wife. On one occasion I had an incorrigibly lazy
dependent working for me; I said to him, 'R., the
Nicobarese are the laziest race I have ever come
across, and you are the laziest Nicobarese I have
ever seen. What does your father-in-law say about
you?' The answer came readily enough. 'He does
not like me to work hard, for it would be bad for
the baby.' Reasoning as the Nicobarese do on
homœopathic principles, if it is bad for the sucking
child when the mother works hard and gets into a
state of profuse perspiration, surely it must after
all be equally bad for the baby if the father should
work hard.

"If the home of the parties is at some considerable distance from the birth-houses, a pregnant
woman and her husband may go, some weeks
before the child is expected, to live in or near
*el-panam* in one of the 'good' (*i.e.* ceremoniously
clean) houses on the beach or in the neighbourhood.
In at least one of the villages, however, the birth-
houses are not side by side with the dead-houses,
much less identical with them, as is not infre-
quently the case, but away by themselves in the
midst of the cocoa-palm grove—much like the
ordinary *tu-hēt* (cluster of houses), only the birth-
houses and neighbourhood were very much worse
kept than any other group of Nicobarese houses
that I have ever seen.

"When the labour pains begin, the woman goes
to one of the birth-huts, for if she gave birth to a

child in a 'good' house, that would become cere-
monially unclean and have to be pulled down and
burnt; no one could live in it again. Some of the
richer Nicobarese families have their own birth-hut
side by side with the others, in order to have some
small degree of privacy. There are always a number
of women and their husbands living in *el-panam*,
for they do not ordinarily leave for their own homes
until perhaps three months after the birth of the
child. . . . If there is any delay in delivery it is
presumed to be due to the child being trapped or
held or nipped by something homœopathically. So,
though diligent search had been made long before
to make sure that no clothes or other belongings of
the parents were shut or boxed up, or contained
any knots, a new search is made, and care is taken
that the door of the hut and the lids of all boxes
near be left open, so that there may be a clear
passage. The man will also lift up an inch or two
the big racing canoes of the village and then put
them back in the same place; and if there were any
logs or other heavy things lying about, they would
lift them up or turn them over in order to lighten
the load of the spirit and to set the infant free.
Similarly, neither a pregnant woman nor her husband should ever make anything tight, as nailing a
board or tying knots, for fear that the spirit of the
unborn infant should get tied up in the knots, and
that, in consequence, there would be a great difficulty, if not impossibility, of delivery when the
time should come. My munshi and interpreter, to
whom I am to a very large extent indebted for
whatever work I have done among the Nicobarese
and for whatever knowledge I may have of them and

their customs, had spent five years of his youth in Burma, and so was not always mindful of his duty according to the lore of the Nicobarese. Finding time hang heavily on his hands, he once began in his leisure hours to make a fishing net, when his parents-in-law reproved him strongly for his gross cruelty in thus foolishly and unthinkingly endangering the life of his wife and his unborn child. . . . The husband looks after his wife, remaining with her in *el-panam* and supplying all her needs.

"When the baby is still under a month old the father must not do any heavy work, nor walk in the sun, nor bathe in the sea, for they do not want the child to get sick (one said to me), thus illustrating the principle of the couvade" (**134**).

These two long and interesting accounts of the couvade and related ideas in the Nicobar Islands throw considerable light on the interpretation of the problem, and they will be discussed in a later section of this book. We must now proceed eastwards and note the occurrences of the customs in the islands of Indonesia. The best account of couvade in this area is to be found in an important paper by the Dutch anthropologist G. A. Wilken (**135**). Roth, without citing the title of this paper nor giving a bibliographical reference to it, has conveniently translated extracts from it into English (**94**, pp. 207-212).

Various forms of couvade occur in the Malay Peninsula. Speaking of the Orang Benu-wa of Malacca and of the Boeginese and Macassarese, Wilken says: "Of the first-named, more especially of the Jakuns, who inhabit the province Johor

along the river Madek, we read that they have the
following superstition which, so long as children
are unable to walk, prevents their parents from
using as food certain fish and animals; as soon as
the little ones have acquired the use of their legs
this restriction is removed, and the parents are
once more able to indulge in what has so long been
*pantang* or forbidden. Should this superstition not
be complied with, and any parent eat of any of the
forbidden creatures during the period of restriction, the children are supposed to be liable to an
illness called *busong*, arising, according to the
Malays, from *pĕrut-Kĕmbung* or swollen stomach.
Concerning the Boeginese and the Macassarese,
these people believe that the man, during the pregnancy of his wife, and she also, often behaves whim-
sically, and has desires, appetites for food which
are not otherwise eaten—a belief, as will presently
appear, that may have had some connection originally with couvade" (135; 94, p. 211; and below, p.143).

On the large island of Sumatra couvade does
not appear to have been recorded, but it occurs on
some of the smaller islands of the Sumatran coast.
With regard to the island of Nias, the father and
mother are both placed under numerous restrictions both before and after the birth of a child.
If any of these restrictions should be contravened
by the mother or by the father, the placenta might
remain in the womb, the child might be still-born
or might suffer some deformity (135; 94, p. 210).
"The anxiety of the father for his unborn child is
very peculiar. It is thought that there is the deepest
sympathy between him and it, and on this account
the father must take the greatest care in what he

does or in what befalls him, as it will affect the child" (102, translated).

In the neighbouring Mentawi Islands the husband is confined to the house for two months, and all work other than necessary fishing is prohibited. The couvade terminates in a feast, and work is then resumed (78, p. 201). In Borneo the Land Dyaks observe a five-day couvade according to some accounts (78, p. 200), or four or eight days according to others. "On these occasions [birth-celebrations] the unfortunate husband seems to be very ill-treated, particularly after the birth, being dieted on rice and salt, and forbidden during four days to bathe or show his face out of doors. The interdict, however, extends to the whole family, who can neither visit or be visited for the space of eight days" (99). "Among the Land Dyaks of Borneo the husband, before the birth of his child, may do no work with a sharp instrument except what is necessary for the farm; nor may he fire guns, nor strike animals, nor do any violent work, lest bad influences should affect the child; and after it is born the father is kept in seclusion indoors for several days, and dieted on rice and salt, to prevent not his own, but the child's stomach from swelling" (124, p. 292; c.f. 98, p. 160).

A kind of "rationalized" couvade, based also on sympathetic magic, is recorded of the Kayans of Borneo by Dr. Charles Hose: "Both the father and the mother observe certain restrictions during the early months and years of the child's life, with diminishing strictness as the child grows older. The general aim of all these restrictions seems to be to establish and maintain about the child a certain atmosphere or, they say, a certain odour, in which alone it can thrive. . . . During the child's infancy neither father nor mother will eat or touch anything the properties of which are thought to be harmful or undesirable for the child, such as the skin of the deer or tiger-cat, and the child himself is still more strictly preserved from such contact" (**47**).

Amongst the Dyaks, another writer has recorded that during pregnancy both the woman and her husband have to observe elaborate food-taboos, and both must abstain from lighting or going near a fire, drilling holes in wood, and immersing themselves. The neglect of these precautions is believed to have an adverse effect upon the embryo and might cause still-birth (**77**; and cf. **177**).

As regards the Philippine Islands, the couvade custom was observed by some of the tribes of the interior of North Luzon, more especially in the province of Bontok (**135; 94**, p. 209). "When a woman has given birth to a child, she must go with it to the river, wash it and herself, and return to the settlement, hand the child over to the father, and go on with her work. She only has it back to give it the breast; the man nurses it, carries it wrapped in a covering on his back, and receives the visits of friends and acquaintances whilst the woman works in the fields" (**100**, translated).

With regard to the Tagals of Luzon, not only the mother, but also the father, have to observe certain rules in regard to their offspring. "He must forbear from the enjoyment of double fruits [*i.e.* fruits which have grown together], otherwise his wife will have twins, which Tagals by no means wish to happen" (**16**, translated).

We have some instances of couvade in the Moluccas and other islands lying between Celebes and New Guinea. "The Alfoeros of Boero must be named first. This is what Schouten, who touched on the island in the middle of the seventeenth century, says of the custom: 'The black woman in her confinement also does not remain in her bed, but henceforth goes with her new-born child to the river, and she, when she has well washed both the child and herself, returns to her usual occupation, and yet no harm follows. Still, besides, I am truly assured, that as the little darkie of the island of Boero begins to thrive a little, from that time forward the man, as husband of the confined woman, very absurdly pretends to be ill, and allows himself to be right handsomely pampered, so that the blockhead is waited upon more than usual. In the meanwhile the black woman must [return] to her work in order to prepare delicacies for her husband, in order to put the poor fellow on his legs again.' This account is confirmed by Captain Van der Hart (44). Those who in 1850 made a voyage round Celebes and to some of the Moluccas met again at Boero with that which W. Schouten had, in his time, come across there. . . . So also the couvade seems still, according to him [Van der Hart], to be practised in the island. 'As soon as a child is born', says he, at least, 'there is not so much trouble made as with us in Europe; the mother immediately after her delivery goes with her child to the river, both wash themselves, and therewith the affair is finished . . . Coming back from the river, the mother goes about her usual duties; the man, on the other hand, behaves sickly (as infirm) and absurdly, as though he had been confined, enjoys with much gusto the delicacies which are prepared for him by his wife'" (135; 94, pp. 207-208).

Roth doubts the authenticity of Van der Hart's account, on the ground that it is almost exactly the same as Schouten's, and this similarity suggests that the one is copied from the other. Wilken, although he himself did not find any evidence of the custom, thinks it likely that it still existed in his time in the north of the island. In any case, we have no reason to doubt Schouten's veracity. Traces of couvade have been recorded from other islands of the Moluccas and neighbouring groups. With regard to the inhabitants of the islands of Leti and Kissner, it is said that when a woman is confined, superstition forbids her husband for some months to dig, plough or hoe (135; 94, p. 208).

Practices similar to those already mentioned are recorded by Wilken from the islands of Timor Laut, where the father at first has to carry and take care of the child, while the mother, after she has bathed, performs her usual housework.

"Amongst the natives of the Uliasers, natives of the Amboynas, we finally see how the man during the pregnancy of his wife is obliged to abstain from a number of things. He is forbidden, so we read [quoting von Schmid, 1843], 'to manu- facture objects such as tables, chairs, doors, win- dows and such like of same nature too, in similar obligation to bring together, to join, or, in order to drive in anywhere, a peg or a nail for fear lest the woman might have a difficulty in labour'.[1] So

[1] [I have not been able to obtain a sight of Von Schmid's work, so am unable to control this rather peculiar translation. W. R. D.]

may he, as is told us later on, not be allowed to
split bamboos, in order, for example, to make a
fish-hook, lest the child have a harelip. Nor is it
with any eye to the child['s welfare] lawful for him
when in sight of the child to open cocoanuts, to cut
hair, or to hold the rudder of a vessel" (**135; 94,**
pp. 208-209).

There is no available evidence apparently of
actual couvade on the mainland of New Guinea,
although some related ideas are to be found.
Chalmers states that at Suau the husband shuts
himself up for some days after the birth of a child,
and abstains from food (**22**), and amongst the
natives of Mouat, according to another writer, the
father before the birth of a child abstains from
certain kinds of food which, it is believed, might
have an effect on the child (**12**). Speaking of con-
finements in British New Guinea, Dr. Seligman
writes: "While his wife is secluded in the house,
the child's father must abstain from chewing betel,
and observe the same food-taboos as his wife under
penalty of his child becoming seriously ill. He does
not avoid his newly born child, nor stay away from
the house; in fact he lives in the house and may see
the child directly it is born. Cohabitation should
not be resumed until the child can toddle about; if
it is resumed before then the child will weaken,
sicken and perhaps die" (**103**). Among the Kiwai
Papuans (Fly River estuary), if a woman is pregnant, both she, and her husband, must refrain from
going near anyone who is ill (**62**). These last instances, whilst not true couvade, have the same
underlying idea.

I can find no record at all of couvade in

Australia, but it reappears once more in the islands
of Melanesia. At San Cristoval, Solomon Islands,
"for two or three weeks after the birth of a child
the father guards himself carefully from the sun
and from the cold wind which comes up nightly
from the river valleys, and from the rain. He is
careful to do no heavy work, and especially not to
carry anything heavy" (37).

Codrington, who also mentions the practice at
San Cristoval, supplies information regarding other
islands in the Melanesian group.

"A proper couvade has perhaps been observed
in San Cristoval alone, when the young father was
found lying-in after the birth of his child; and it
should be observed that this was where the child
follows the father's kindred. There is much, however, which approaches this. At Saa [Malanta,
Solomons] it is not only the expectant mother who
is careful what she eats, the father also both before
and after the child's birth refrains from some kinds
of food which would hurt the child. He will not
eat pig's flesh, and he abstains from the movements
which are believed to do harm, upon the principle
that the father's movements affect those of the
child. A man will not do hard work, lift heavy
weights, or go out to sea; he keeps quiet lest the
child should start, should overstrain itself, or
should throw itself about as he paddles. In the
Banks Islands also, both parents are careful what
they eat when the child is born, they take only
what if taken by the infant would not make it ill;
before the birth of her first child the mother must
not eat fish caught by the hook, net, or trap. After
the birth of the first child, the father does no heavy

work for a month; after the birth of any of his children he takes care not to go into those sacred places, *tano rongo*, into which the child could not go without risk. It is the same in the New Hebrides; the expectant Araga father keeps away from the sacred places, *ute sapuga*, before the child's birth, and does not enter his house; after the birth, he does work in looking after his wife and child, but he must not eat shell-fish and other produce of the beach, for the infant would suffer from ulcers if he did. In Leper's Island the father is very careful for ten days; he does no work, will not climb a tree, or go far into the sea to bathe, for if he exerts himself the child will suffer. If during this time he goes to any distance, as to the beach, he brings back with him a little stone representing the infant's soul, which may have followed him; arrived at his home, he cries, 'Come hither,' and puts down the stone in the house; then he waits till the child sneezes, and he cries, 'Here it is,' knowing then that the soul has not been lost" (23).

With reference to the Banks Islands, Rivers gives some further particulars: "The parents must remain in the house for some time after the child is born. The father must not do any work for five days (till the cord has separated) and he must not do any hard work for a hundred days. He must not eat food which comes from a place where the people have been doing an *oloolo* rite [a magical ceremony described on p. 156], nor must he go to such a place himself. If by any chance this happened, he would have to submit to a ceremony to remove the source of danger to the child" (88).

In New Ireland, when a woman is confined, her husband, in order to rid her of the pains of delivery, goes to the men's club-house, where he lies down and feigns suffering, writhing in imaginary pain. This is continued until the child is born (75).

# CHAPTER VI

## THE COUVADE IN AMERICA

QUITE isolated geographically is the record of a form of couvade in Greenland. Here it is stated that on the birth of a child the husbands "must forbear working for some weeks, neither must they drive any trade during that time" (34).

In North America couvade seems to be confined to California; I have been unable to find any record of the custom elsewhere in the Northern Continent.[1] In California, after the birth of a child, the women "went about their duties as usual, and in other particulars observe no manner of caution, going to the forest for wood and food, and performing every other service the husband wanted; while he in the meantime lay in his cave, or stretched at full length under a tree, affecting to be extremely weak and ill; and this farce continued for three or four days" (129).

Writing of the Central Californians, Bancroft says: "When childbirth overtakes the wife, the husband puts himself to bed, and there, grunting and groaning, affects to suffer all the agonies of a woman in labour. Lying there, he is nursed and

[1] It seems probable, however, that a trace of the custom has survived in Ontario. See **93**.

tended for some days as carefully as though he were the actual sufferer" (**8**, p. 391).

In Southern California the husband did not lie-in, but was placed under certain restrictions. He was not allowed to leave the house, nor to eat fish or meat (**8**, p. 412). Similarly, amongst the Lagunero and Ahomana (New Mexico), the husbands ate neither fish nor meat, and went to bed for six or seven days (**8**, p. 585).

Central and South America provide many instances of couvade, and the literature of the subject has recently been enriched by a good discussion of the custom in that continent by Dr. Karsten (**52**). This writer gives good reason for thinking that the custom is not, or was not, so restricted as many writers would have us believe (*e.g.* **52**). It seems very probable that originally, at least, the custom was distributed over almost the entire continent. From the statement of Bridges (**18**) it seems probable that couvade was originally practised in the extreme south by the Fuegians. He states that among the Jahgans "the mother and father of a newly born child . . . are both careful as regards their food, thinking some kinds are hurtful to the child. They generally also keep quiet for a week or two after the child's birth." This certainly appears to be a custom derived from couvade, and other writers state that a fully developed couvade exists amongst the Fuegians (**55**), but, unfortunately, no details are available.

The custom was evidently prominent during the seventeenth and eighteenth centuries, as many writers, mostly missionaries, have left us accounts of it; and although there is a tendency for the couvade to disappear, it is still maintained in many districts.

Rochefort (89) and Du Tertré (115) have given a full account of couvade as practised by the Caribs of the West Indies. This has been conveniently summarized by Tylor, whose account is here quoted. "When a child is born, the mother goes presently to her work, but the father begins to complain, and takes to his hammock, and there he is visited as though he were sick, and undergoes a course of dieting which would cure of the gout 'the most replete of Frenchmen. How they can fast so much and not die of it', continues the narrator, 'is amazing to me, for they sometimes pass the five first days without eating or drinking anything; then up to the tenth they drink *oüycou*, which has about as much nourishment in it as beer. These ten days passed, they begin to eat cassava only, drinking *oüycou*, and abstaining from everything else for the space of a whole month. During this time, however, they only eat the inside of the cassava, so that what is left is like the rim of a hat when the block has been taken out, and all these cassava rims they keep for the feast at the end of forty days, hanging them up in the house with a cord. When the forty days are up they invite their relations and best friends, who being arrived, before they set to eating, hack the skin of this poor wretch with agouti-teeth, and draw blood from all parts of his body, in such sort that from being sick by pure imagination they often make a real patient of him. This is, however, so to speak, only the fish, for now comes the sauce they prepare for him; they take sixty or eighty large grains of pimento or Indian pepper, the strongest they can get, and after well mashing it in water, they wash with this peppery infusion the wounds and scars of the poor fellow, who, I believe, suffers no less than if he were burnt alive; however, he must not utter a single word if he will not pass for a coward and a wretch. This ceremony finished, they bring him back to his bed, where he remains some days more, and the rest go and make good cheer in the house at his expense. Nor is this all, for through the space of six whole months he eats neither birds nor fish, firmly believing that this would injure the child's stomach, and that it would participate in the natural faults of the animals on which its father had fed; for example, if the father ate turtle, the child would be deaf and have no brains like this animal, if he ate manati the child would have little round eyes like this creature, and so on with the rest' " (124, pp. 288-289).

The couvade custom is practised in the Pearl Islands, in the Gulf of Panama (78, p. 204).

Richard Schomburgk states (of the Macusis of Guiana) that after the birth of the child, the father suspends his hammock by the side of that of his wife, and is confined with her, until the navel-string of the child falls off. During this time neither the father nor mother must do any kind of work, nor handle weapons, nor bathe. Their only food is cassava and their sole drink warm water. The father is not allowed to scratch himself with his nails, and for this purpose he is provided with a slip of wood taken from the midrib of a palm. The violation of this injunction would bring sickliness upon the child (101, pp. 313-314).

A more recent account of the couvade among the

Guiana Indians is given by Sir Everard im Thurn. "This custom, which is common to the uncivilized people of many parts of the world, is probably amongst the strangest ever invented by the human brain. Even before the child is born, the father abstains for a time from certain kinds of animal food. The woman works as usual up to a few hours before the birth of the child. At last she retires alone, or accompanied only by some other women, to the forest, where she ties up her hammock; and then the child is born. Then in a few hours—often less than a day—the woman, who like all women living in a very unartificial condition, suffers but little, gets up and resumes her ordinary work. . . . In all cases where the matter came under my notice, the mother left her hammock almost at once. In any case, no sooner is the child born than the father takes to his hammock, and, abstaining from every sort of work, from meat and all other food, except a weak gruel of cassava meal, from smoking, from washing himself, and, above all, from touching weapons of any sort, is nursed and cared for by all the women of the place. One other regulation, mentioned by Schomburgk, is certainly quaint; the interesting father may not scratch himself with his finger-nails, but he may use for this purpose a splinter, specially provided, from the midrib of a cockerite palm.[1]

[1] [The prohibition of scratching with the finger-nails occurs elsewhere in other ceremonies. Thus in Queensland during the ceremonies of rain-making, the men "scratch the tops of their heads and the inside of their shins from time to time with twigs; if they were to scratch themselves with their fingers alone, they believe that the whole effect of the ceremony would be spoiled" (Frazer, *The Golden Bough*, 3rd ed. vol. i. p. 254). Scratching

"Couvade is such a widespread institution, that I had often read and wondered at it; but it was not until I saw it practised around me, and found that I was often deprived of the services of my best hunters or boat-hands by the necessity which they felt, and which nothing could persuade them to disregard, that I realized its full strangeness" (119).

The custom of couvade as practised by the Arawaks of Dutch Guiana has been described by several writers, notably Quandt (82) and Firmin (36). After the birth of a child, the father must fire no gun, hunt no large game and fell no tree. He may stay near home and hunt little birds with bow and arrow and angle for small fish. Quandt takes the view that the man, being deprived of his usual occupations, and finding the time weigh heavily on his hands, takes to his hammock from sheer *ennui*!

When describing the Carib couvade of the West Indies (above, p. 93), reference was made to the avoidance by the father of certain animals because of their supposed effect upon the child. In this connection, the following account is of special interest:

"Some of the *men* of the Acawois and Caribi nations, when they have reason to expect an increase in their families, consider themselves bound to abstain from certain kinds of meat, lest the expected child should in some mysterious way

---

with the fingers is prohibited to a girl at her first menstruation in the Torres Straits Islands and amongst numerous tribes of Indians both of North and of South America (*ibid.* vol. x. pp. 38, 39, 41, 42, 44, 47, 50, 53, 92). In such cases a special piece of wood or some other implement is provided for the purpose. See also *ibid.* vol. iii. p. 146.]

be injured by *their* partaking of it. The *Acouri* (or Agouti) is thus tabooed, lest, like that little animal, the child should be meagre; the *Haimara* also, lest it should be blind, the outer coating of the eye of that fish suggesting film or cataract; the *Labba*, lest the infant's mouth should protrude like the labba's, or lest it be spotted like the labba, which spots would ultimately become ulcers; the *Marudi* is also forbidden, lest the infant be still-born, the screeching of that bird being considered ominous of death. Both the above tribes and the Waraus consider it their duty to abstain from venison *after* their wives are confined, lest the child on arriving at manhood be found wanting in speed, exemplified by the slow pace which the female deer when she has a young fawn at her feet is obliged to observe. Such are some of the dietetic rules laid down for the *men* by their system of superstition. They are probably observed by very few in their full vigour, for the forbidden animals form a large proportion of the Indian's bill of fare as found in the forests, and a Carib or other polygamist with three or four wives might be debarred from tasting them during the whole, or the best period, of his manhood" (**17**, p. 355; **94**, p. 220).

The same writer, speaking of actual couvade amongst the same tribes, gives the following instance: "An instance of this custom came under my own observation; when the man in robust health, without a single bodily ailment, was lying in his hammock in the most provoking manner, and carefully and respectfully attended by the women; while the mother of the new-born infant was cooking— none apparently regarding her" (**17**, p. 101).

Amongst the Wapiana, when a woman has given birth to a child, she sits with her infant on the ground, while her husband builds a hut over her. He divides off a portion of the hut, and there observes the couvade (**78**, p. 203).

The Bakaïri of the Xingu River district have a couvade that lasts a month, and the father of a child among the Ipurinas of Bolivia abstains from eating the flesh of the tapir till his child is a year old (**78**, p. 204).

Writing of the Petivares of Brazil in the seventeenth century (1633), Laët says: "Quand les femmes Petivares sont accouchées, les maris se couchent au lit et sont salués courtoisement de tous leur voisins et sont traités des femmes soigneusement et largement" (**60**).

Southey makes the following reference to the couvade in Brazil: "Immediately upon a woman's delivery the father takes to his hammock, covers himself up, and is nurst there till the navel-string of the infant has dried away; the union between him and his progeny is regarded as so intimate that the utmost care must be taken of him lest the child should suffer" (**107**).

Spix and Martius make several allusions to couvade and related customs. They relate that bleeding is practised amongst the Indians of Rio Yupurá, especially during pregnancy. Not only the wives but also the husbands are bled, and the same practice is followed among the Botocudos (**109**, p. 1821). The country on the lower part of the River Içá (which has its source in the N.W. in the Cordillera, where it is called Putumayo) is inhabited chiefly by tribes of the Passé and the Jurí.

Among the Passé, after the birth of a child, both
father and mother remain in the dark for a month
and eat nothing but mandiocca. During this time
the father blackens himself and stays in his hammock. Among the Jurí, as so often elsewhere, the
father lies in his hammock and the mother waits
upon him (109, p. 1186). This couvade is kept up
until the child's navel-string falls off, about eight
days (68, vol. i. p. 511). The Mundzucú are a poly-
gamous tribe. Like the Caribs and the Tupé, when
a child is born the father lies in his hammock for
several weeks. He is waited on by the mother and
visited by the neighbours. The reason is that the
child is attributed to the father alone, the mother
being regarded as the soil which receives the seed
(109, p. 339).

In Peru, von Tschudi states vaguely, the husband, after the birth of a child, goes to bed for a few
weeks (123).

With regard to the Coroados of Brazil, Spix and
Martius report that "as soon as the woman is
evidently pregnant, or has been delivered, the man
withdraws. A strict regimen is observed before the
birth; the man and the woman refrain from the
flesh of certain animals, and live chiefly on fish and
fruits" (110).

Amongst some tribes, the husbands do not lie-
in, but fast with their wives for various periods
(109, p. 381; 68, pp. 427, 441, 482). In the case of
the Coimbas of Peru, the husband does not go to
bed, but sits motionless at his door during his
wife's confinement, and remains until the child has
been washed and its sex announced to him (97).

Another seventeenth-century writer, Biet, describing the couvade says that as soon as a woman is pregnant, her husband at once abstains from eating the larger fishes and turtles, and avoids those who catch them for fear that his wife's soul, his own, and those of his children should enter the fishes. After delivery of the wife, the husband takes to his bed for six weeks, and, instead of tending his wife, the latter waits upon him. He avoids the gaze of his neighbours and meets them with downcast eyes. He eats so little, that when at length his six weeks' penance is finished, he is as thin as a skeleton (14).[1]

The Jivaro Indians of Ecuador and the Piojés of the Putumayo both practise the couvade custom. "The couvade is rife among the Jivaros; and at the birth of a child, the mother has to undergo all her parturient troubles outside the house, exposed to the elements, whilst the husband quietly reclines in the house, coddling and dieting himself for some days until he has recovered from the shock produced upon his system by the increased weight of his responsibilities as a father. This custom is still in some measure extant in many of the civilized villages on the Solomons, where, amongst the Tapuyos and even degrees more approached to the whites, the father, on the birth of a son or daughter, lays himself in the hammock, from which he will not move on any consideration to do any kind of work, nor especially to touch any cutting instrument, fearing thereby to exercise evil influences upon the healthy development of the child" (105).

"Another very curious custom is that of both

---

[1] I have not been able to see this work, and do not know, therefore, what part of South America it relates to. The above is an epitome of the French text printed by Roth (94, p. 219).

father and mother fasting for days after the birth of a child. Sometimes this is kept up so long that it is a wonder that at least the mother does not sink under the debilitating ordeal. If the father is away from his wife he also fasts three days on hearing the news that she has borne him a child, as some of the Piojés assured me" (104).

The Austrian Jesuit missionary, Martin Dobrizhoffer (1717–1791), who worked for eighteen years among the Guaranis and Abipones, has given an interesting account of the couvade custom as practised by the latter. The Abipones are an equestrian tribe in central South America, between Santa Fé and St. Iago, Paraguay. Dobrizhoffer's narrative is in Latin,[1] and I accordingly quote Tylor's translation: "No sooner do you hear that the wife has borne a child, than you will see the Abipone husband lying in bed, huddled up with mats and skins lest some ruder breath of air should touch him, fasting, kept in private, and for a number of days abstaining religiously from certain viands; you would swear it was he who had had the child. . . . I had read about this in old times, and laughed at it, never thinking I could believe such madness, and I used to suspect that this barbarian custom was related more in jest than in earnest; but at last I saw it with my own eyes in use among the Abipones. And in truth they observe this ancestral

---

[1] The full title of Dobrizhoffer's book is too long to insert in the Bibliography. It reads: *Historia de Abiponibus, Equestri Bellicosaque Paraguariae Natione, locupletata Copiosis Barbararum Gentium, Urbium, Fluminum, Ferarum, Amphibiorum, Insectorum, Serpentium praecipuorum, Piscium, Avium, Arborum, Plantarum aliarumque ejusdem Provinciae Proprietatum Observationibus.*

custom, troublesome as it is, the more willingly
and diligently from their being altogether per-
suaded that the sobriety and quiet is effectual for
the well-being of the new-born offspring, and is
even necessary. Hear, I pray, a confirmation of this
matter. Francisco Barreda, Deputy of the Royal
Governor of Tucuman, came to visit the new
colony of Conceiçam, in the territory of Santiago.
To him, as he was walking with me in the court-
yard, the Cacique Malakin came up to pay his
respects, having just left his bed, to which he had
been confined in consequence of his wife's recent
delivery. As I stood by, Barreda offered the Cacique
a pinch of Spanish snuff, but seeing the savage
refuse it contrary to custom, he thought he must
be out of his mind, for he knew him at other times
to be greedy of this nasal delicacy; so he asked me
aside to inquire the cause of his abstinence. I asked
him in the Abiponian tongue (for this Barreda was
ignorant of, as the Cacique was of Spanish) why he
refused his snuff to-day. 'Don't you know', he
answered, 'that my wife has just been confined?
Must not I, therefore, abstain from stimulating
my nostrils? What a danger my sneezing would
bring upon my child!' No more, but he went back
to his hut to lie down again diligently, lest the
tender little infant should take some harm if he
stayed any longer with us in the open air. For they
believe that the father's carelessness influences the
new-born offspring from a natural bond of sympathy of both. Hence, if the child comes to a
premature end, its death is attributed by the women
to the father's intemperance, this or that cause
being assigned; he did not abstain from mead; he

had loaded his stomach with water-hog; he had swum across the river when the air was chilly; he had neglected to shave off his long eyebrows; he had devoured underground honey, stamping on the bees with his feet; he had ridden till he was tired and sweated. With raving like this the crowd of women accuse the father with impunity of causing the child's death, and are accustomed to pour curses on the unoffending husband" (31 *apud* 124, pp. 290-291.)

Finally, in the case of the Chiriguanos Indians, of the Pilcomayo River district (Paraguay), not only the father but the children also lie-in and fast at the birth of each successive child (118).[1]

1 See the further remarks on couvade in America, below, p. 144.

# CHAPTER VII

### THE GEOGRAPHICAL DISTRIBUTION OF COUVADE

In discussing the geographical distribution of couvade, it must be kept in mind that we are dealing with a custom that leaves no visible or tangible trace of its existence. We can trace the diffusion of megalithic monuments, for instance, because the megaliths themselves remain as permanent witnesses of the peoples or of the civilizations that erected them. Mummification again, whilst affording a less complete chain of evidence, has, nevertheless, provided the material for distributional study in the form of actual mummies from many widely separated localities, the technique of which can be examined, and the same may be said of the custom of artificially deforming the skull. Even tattooing and ear-piercing are customs that leave evidence of their ancient practice in statues and pictures. For all these customs we have, besides such tangible proofs, written history and oral tradition, but for couvade we have to rely entirely on the latter. Our material, therefore, must be to some extent incomplete, for couvade may have been practised in certain localities for which we have no written records, and since it is a custom that tends to disappear before the influence of the white man, it may be vanishing, or has already vanished, from many places that do not happen to have come under the trained observation of anthropological science.

From the records of history, tradition or observation that have been enumerated in the foregoing chapters, we can perceive that the distribution of couvade constitutes a more or less definite chain, although from many parts of it links are missing. It will be observed that the recorded localities in which couvade is, or has been, practised correspond to a remarkable degree with those associated with megalithic monuments and with customs usually connected with what has conveniently been called the heliolithic culture-complex, a complex comprising many curious customs and beliefs, amongst which may be specially mentioned sun-worship, mummification, ear-piercing, tattooing and cranial deformation.[1]

I do not propose on this occasion to enter into any discussion of the general question of the diffusion of culture, but the inherent strangeness of the custom of couvade (no less than of the other customs referred to) makes it impossible to believe that it originated independently in the various

[1] The distribution of mummification has been discussed by Prof. G. Elliot Smith in his *Migrations of Early Culture* (Manchester, 1915); that of tattooing by Miss A. W. Buckland, *Journ. of the Anthropological Inst.* vol. xvii. (1888), pp. 318-328, with Pl. vi. (map), and more recently by W. D. Hambly, *The History of Tattooing and its Significance*, London, 1925; of ear-piercing by J. Park Harrison, *Journ. of the Anthropological Inst.* vol. ii. (1872), pp. 190-198. A sketch-map giving the general outline of the distribution of these and other customs will be found in Prof. Elliot Smith's memoir, p. 14, and in that of Hambly, facing p. 25.

places in which it has been recorded. In many of these places there is the clearest proof of contact derived from a variety of evidence, and the existence of so curious a custom in widely separated localities throws the onus of proof, it seems to me, *a priori* on those who allege that it originated spontaneously in each of such places. The association of couvade with many other practices that follow the same routes seems to point to its origin, with them, in the ancient civilizations of the Eastern Mediterranean area.

Speaking of the geographical distribution of the many curious customs that make up the heliolithic complex, Professor Elliot Smith has written: "It will be found that in most respects the areas in which this extraordinary assortment of bizarre customs and beliefs is found coincide one with the other. In some of the series gaps occur, which probably are more often due to lack of information on our part than to real absence of the practice; in other places one or other of the elements of this complex culture-mixture has overflowed the common channel and broken into new territory. But considered in conjunction, these data enable us definitely and precisely to map out the route taken by this peculiarly distinctive group of eccentricities of the human mind. If each of them is considered alone there are many breaks in the chain and many uncertainties as to the precise course; but when taken together, all of these gaps are bridged" (**108**, p. 3).[1]

[1] The whole of the introductory part of this memoir, which deals with the distribution of the practice of mummification in particular, should be carefully read, as it throws much light on the

The distribution of other customs usually found in association with couvade, but which have no genetic connection with it, will help us to trace the diffusion of the custom in places for which our records are deficient or wanting.

There is quite definite evidence that mummification originated in Egypt in early times (probably under the First Dynasty); tattooing may have been practised in Egypt before the First Dynasty, but it was certainly in vogue in the Eleventh Dynasty, as actual mummies of that period, on whose skins patterns are tattooed, have been found. Piercing of the ear-lobe was practised in Egypt certainly as early as the Seventeenth Dynasty, and we have evidence of cranial deformation in the Eighteenth. In view of these facts, one naturally looks for the origin of couvade in the same country, but there is absolutely no evidence of its occurrence there. What we know of the manners and customs of the ancient Egyptians is derived from a study of their wall-paintings, from such hints as the popular literature conveys, and from the accounts of Greek travellers, chiefly Herodotus and Diodorus Siculus. The Egyptians themselves have left us no written account of their daily practices as such. We have no native account of so cardinal a custom as mummification, for instance; what we know is derived from the accounts of the Greek historians and from the observation of actual mummies. One would therefore hardly expect to find any Egyptian account of

question of the diffusion of customs in general. Since it was published (in 1915) much additional and confirmatory evidence has been forthcoming.

the couvade (if it had been a usual custom in the country), but one would expect, if it had been practised, to find some mention of it by Herodotus or by Diodorus Siculus. Whilst, therefore, there is no evidence whatever that the Egyptians observed the couvade custom, there is at the same time no positive evidence against the possibility that it may have been observed. Even if many of the customs in the heliolithic complex are of Egyptian origin, it does not follow that they all are. Closely associated with the heliolithic track is the widespread tradition of the destruction of mankind by a deluge, but this tradition originated not in Egypt, but in Mesopotamia.[1]

In the entire absence of evidence, therefore, I make no suggestion that couvade originated in Egypt, and its origin must be sought in one of the neighbouring lands of the ancient world. That couvade is an ancient custom we know from the fact that it is mentioned by classical writers—Strabo, Diodorus, Plutarch, Apollonius and Valerius Flaccus, and it is probably more ancient than the time of the earliest of these writers. A form of couvade was practised in Cyprus (admitting for the moment that the custom mentioned by Plutarch may be classed as couvade, a point that will be discussed in the next chapter), and it is quite probable that Cyprus may have been its place of

[1] The flood stories of the world have been conveniently collected by Sir James Frazer, *Folk-Lore in the Old Testament* (London, 1918), vol. i. pp. 104-361.

The Egyptians had a legend of the destruction of mankind, but the god punished his rebellious subjects by slaughter and not by flood. This point is further discussed in the Addenda; see below, p. 145.

origin. Assuming this to be the case merely for the sake of argument, we will trace its movement from that centre.

Passing westwards, the first large island encountered is Crete, and it is probable that the Cyprian custom was followed here, for the cult of Theseus and Ariadne is closely associated with Crete. We have as yet no evidence, however, that couvade was known in that island. We can assert with some certainty that it was unknown on the mainland of Greece, because three Greek writers record couvade as a strange custom in foreign lands. Had the couvade been familiar to these writers, they would scarcely have noted it as an oddity when they came across it elsewhere. The same may be said of Italy and Sicily, but couvade reappears once more in Corsica (30). I can find no evidence of it in Sardinia,[1] but it survived until recent times in the Balearic Islands (6). Reaching Northern Spain, we have Strabo's record of the custom (1st century A.D.) and the testimony of other writers of its survival in later times (see above, p. 58). Thence the custom spread through France, probably under Celtic influence, into Germany on the west, and to the British Isles on the north.

Returning now to Cyprus, we have to trace the distribution of the custom southwards to Africa. Here our material is defective. We know that there was intercourse between Cyprus and Egypt certainly as early as the New Empire, and if couvade originated in Cyprus, the custom must have been carried up the Nile. It has left no trace of its

---

[1] Roth, on the authority of Tylor, states definitely that couvade does *not* occur in Sardinia (**94**, p. 207). See, however, below, p.141.

existence in Egypt or in Nubia, but we find—not a complete couvade, but its underlying motive— in the region of the White Nile and in the district of Mount Elgon. From the Southern Soudan we can trace (by the presence of associated customs) a cultural track south of the Sahara to west coast, and in the Congo basin we have a fully developed couvade custom amongst the Bushongo, a tribe that is believed to have migrated southwards from the edge of the Sahara, near Lake Tchad. The relative rarity of couvade from Africa must probably be ascribed rather to our lack of information than to the real absence of the custom, because we have well-marked cultural routes in Africa over which mummification, ear-piercing, tattooing and other customs follow in close association. The principal stream which followed the Nile Valley branches in several directions in the Southern Soudan, whilst a maritime route can be traced along the Red Sea littoral, through the Bab el-Mandeb and across the Persian Gulf to the Malabar coast of India.

And now as regards Asia. We have only one record of couvade in Western Asia, and that is among the Tibareni of Pontus, south of the Black Sea. From the distribution of other customs we may infer that couvade probably spread here by a route round the coast of Asia Minor. Whether it spread overland to Northern India and Assam from this point, we have no means of knowing. We find couvade, however, in many places on the Malabar coast of India, and it is probable that it thus came by sea across the Persian Gulf. From the western coast the custom spread into Central India, and by two other streams northward and southward. We have records of the custom from Assam and from Chinese Turkestan. From this point, northwards, there is a break in the chain until Japan is reached; probably (from the evidence of distribution afforded by other customs) couvade followed a route round the China coast. From Japan to Kamchatka couvade probably travelled by a route mapped out by other customs, a route that passed through the Aleutian Islands to Alaska. In these latter places, however, we have no evidence of the couvade custom.

Returning to India, we find evidence of a culture stream around the Bay of Bengal through Assam and Burma to the Malay Peninsula and probably also a sea-route to the Nicobar Islands, and thence to Indonesia. For the Nicobars we, fortunately, have full information, but there seems to be no record of true couvade in the Andamans, although it has been observed that the husband of a pregnant woman abstains from eating iguana and *Paradoxurus* (a small carnivorous mammal), believing that the unborn child would suffer if he ate them.[1] Couvade reappears in the island of Nias and in the Mentawi group off the south-western Sumatran coast, and in the Malay Peninsula on the north, although I can find no record of the custom on the mainland of Sumatra itself. In Borneo, in the Celebes and the Philippine Islands couvade occurs, also in some of the smaller islands that lie between

[1] E. H. Man, "The Aboriginal Inhabitants of the Andaman Islands", *Journ. of the Anthropological Inst.* vol. xii. (1883), p. 354. Elsewhere (*ibid.* p. 87) Man states that couvade is quite unknown to the Andamanese.

Celebes and New Guinea. In various parts of New Guinea itself the couvade motive is to be found, although there is apparently no record of any fully developed instance of the custom. In Melanesia couvade is found in some of the smaller islands, as well as in the New Ireland, Solomon and Banks groups, but we are entirely without records of its occurrence in any of the Oceanic islands between Melanesia and the American coast.[1] From Australia also the couvade seems to be entirely absent; the nearest approach to it that I have come across is the custom practised by the Kaitish tribe of Central Australia. Here, it is stated, "the father of a new-born child goes out into the scrub for three days, away from his camp, leaving his girdle and arm-bands behind him, so that he has nothing tied tightly round any part of his body. This freedom from constriction is supposed to benefit his wife."[2]

As we have already seen, couvade has an extensive range in America, and in every case but two (those of Greenland and of Tierra del Fuego) its recorded localities are directly in, or within the

[1] A reminiscence of the couvade may possibly have survived in the remarkable play acted by the natives of Ulieta (Society Islands) for the entertainment of Captain Cook and his officers in 1774. This drama was called *Mididij Harramy* ("The Child is Coming"), and "it concluded with the representation of a woman in labour, acted by a set of great brawny fellows, one of whom at last brought forth a strapping boy, about six feet high, who ran about the stage, dragging after him a large wisp of straw, which hung by a string from his middle".—*Captain Cook's Voyages of Discovery* (Everyman ed.), p. 175.

[2] J. G. Frazer, *The Golden Bough*, 3rd ed. vol. iii. *Taboo and the Perils of the Soul*, p. 295.

influence of, the heliolithic track. What connection culturally there may have been between Greenland and the mainland is but little known, but that such a connection at some time existed is suggested by the fact that the custom of tattooing is also found there and likewise the legend of a Great Flood, whilst tattooing occurs on the opposite side of Davis Straits, which probably marks the northern extent of a culture-stream passing upwards from Lake Superior. The possible survival of tradition in Ontario (**93**) would support this hypothesis.

In North America the recorded range of couvade is not extensive, being confined mainly to California,[1] but in the southern continent the custom has a wide range. It is found in some of the islands of the West Indies, and in Colombia, Venezuela, Guiana, Ecuador, Brazil, Bolivia, Peru and Paraguay. Dr. Kunike, speaking of the distribution of couvade in South America, believes the northern part of South America, especially Brazil and Guiana, to be its principal centres, from whence he believes the custom spread to some few peoples in the northern continent, and that its occurrence elsewhere in America is confined to a few isolated peoples, such as the Abipones of Paraguay. On the other hand, Dr. Karsten considers this account to have but little value, "as it rather shows us where the couvade has been observed by travellers in South America than where it really exists. That it is most common in the Amazonian territories probably is due only to the fact that there are more Indian tribes in the northern parts of the continent than in the south, and also to the

[1] See, however, **93**; and **52**, p. 438, note 4.

fact that the peoples in the deep and inaccessible virgin forests naturally have remained less affected by the levelling influence of civilization than the rest. As to Chaco, the couvade has certainly not been an exceptional phenomenon amongst the Abipones and sundry other tribes. Thus, it has no doubt been practised by the whole great Guaycurú group to which the Abipones belonged. Among the Tobas in Bolivia I have myself found, if not the actual custom of male-childbed, at any rate ideas intimately associated with it. The same holds good of the Mataco-Noctenes, who also know a sort of couvade; and among the Chorotis it exists nearly in its most typical and original form (52, p. 437).

It has generally been asserted that couvade was not practised in the far south, and that the Jahgans and the Onas know nothing of the custom. There seems to be good reason to believe, however, that couvade actually does, or did, exist amongst the Fuegians (18; 52). Similarly, the absence to-day of couvade in the Andean regions of Peru and Bolivia may be due, as Karsten points out, merely to the influence of European civilization, and there is reason for thinking that the practice formerly prevailed (52, p. 438). As, indeed, couvade is elsewhere associated with megalithic culture, mummification, tattooing and cranial deformation, we should expect to find it in the Andean regions of Peru and Bolivia, where all these customs have left definite traces of their former existence.

This brief sketch of the geographical distribution of couvade shows that it comes within the limits of the heliolithic sphere of influence as

usually laid down.[1] Greenland and the extreme
south of South America are both outside the generally defined limit of the ultimate spread of culture
from its original "home". If the very probable
opinion be accepted that couvade was known to the
Fuegians, the limit must be extended southwards
so as to take in the whole of South America. Greenland, however, presents greater difficulties, as the
limit of influence (except on the Pacific coast) is
not considered to extend further northward than
Lake Superior. Whilst the distribution of the
custom of tattooing, and presumably also of other
cultural elements, can be followed in a northerly
direction from Lake Superior towards Davis
Straits between Hudson Bay and the Great Slave
Lake, the chain is incomplete so far as our present
knowledge goes. It would therefore be rash to push
conclusions too far in support either of diffusion or
its converse on the strength of a single record of
couvade in Greenland. Until fuller information is
at our disposal, it is wiser to offer no opinion on
the matter.[2]

To the writer it seems inherently improbable
that so distinctive and curious a custom as couvade
should have originated independently in various
parts of the world. In spite of the incomplete state
of the evidence, the probabilities of the diffusion of
the custom seem to outweigh greatly those of its
independent origin, apart altogether from the facts
suggested by the distribution of other customs with

[1] See the map in *Evolution in the Light of Modern Knowledge*
(London, 1925), facing p. 312.
[2] See the map facing p. 25 of Hambley, *History of Tattooing
and its Significance* (London, 1925).

which couvade is so often found in association. The independent origin theory, however, has been dogmatically asserted by many writers.[1] The custom of couvade by itself is inadequate to prove the hypothesis of diffusion; it must be considered merely as one unit in the extensive complex of which it forms a part, and due allowance must be made for the local factors which preserve or destroy (as the case may be) the evidence or tradition of the former existence of customs and beliefs.

In this connection, it will be useful to quote a few paragraphs from an essay, published in 1922, by the late Dr. Rivers:

"It was assumed as an essential part of the general framework of the science [of anthropology] that, after the original dispersal of mankind, or possibly owing to the independent evolution of different main varieties of Man, large portions of the earth had been cut off from intercourse with others, so that the process of evolution had taken place independently. When similarities, even in minute points of detail, were found in these regions, supposed to have been wholly isolated from one another, it was held that they were due to the uniformity in the constitution of the human mind which, working on similar lines, had brought forth similar products, whether in social organisation, religion, or material culture.

"The adherents of the recent movement to which I have referred [*i.e.* the Diffusionist School] regard the whole of this construction with its main supports of mental uniformity and orderly sequence as built upon the sand. It is claimed that there has

[1] *E.g.* **54**; **64**; **132**, etc.

been no such isolation of one part of the earth from another as has been assumed by the advocates of independent evolution, but that the means of navigation have been capable, for far longer periods than has been supposed, of carrying Man to any part of the earth. The widespread similarities of culture are, it is held, due in the main, if not wholly, to the spread of customs and institutions from some centre in which local conditions specially favoured their development."[1]

[1] W. H. R. Rivers, *History and Ethnology* (London, 1922), pp. 4-5.

# CHAPTER VIII

## THE SIGNIFICANCE OF COUVADE

WE now come to grips with the most difficult aspect of the curious custom, the distribution and variations of which have been outlined in the foregoing chapters—What is the significance of Couvade? Many attempts have been made to explain the meaning of the custom, and these attempts are of very unequal value. Some of them are entitled to the fullest consideration, others are fantastic and absurd. The latter we will deal with first, merely for their historical interest, for they have no other claim that entitles them to be drawn out once more into the light of day from their well-deserved oblivion (see also below, p.146).

When Tylor first published his *Early History of Mankind* (124) in 1865, Professor F. Max Müller contributed to a contemporary journal an essay on manners and customs that was reprinted two years later in the second volume of his *Chips from a German Workshop* (72). In this essay long extracts from Tylor's evidence on couvade were quoted verbatim (without references or even inverted commas); and in singular defiance of the recorded facts, Max Müller proposed feminine tyranny, or " henpecking", as the explanation of the custom. This fantastic theory was supported by such statements as these: "Now, without exaggerating the treatment which a husband receives among ourselves at the time of his wife's confinement, not only from mothers-in-law, sisters-in-law and other female relatives, but from nurses, from every consequential maidservant in the house, it cannot be denied that whilst his wife is suffering, his impunity from pain is generally remarked upon, and if anything goes wrong for which it is possible to blame him, he is sure to hear of it. . . . And would it not be best for him to take to his bed at once and not get up till all is well over?" (72, p. 277). After some further quotations from Tylor, Max Müller proceeds: "The statements, such as they are, given by unprejudiced observers, seem to support very strongly the natural explanation which we proposed of the couvade. It is clear that the poor husband was at first tyrannized over by his female relations, and afterwards frightened into superstition. He began to make a martyr of himself till he made himself really ill, or took to his bed in self-defence. Strange and absurd as the couvade appears at first sight, there is something in it with which, we believe, most mothers-in-law can sympathize; and if we consider that it has been proved to exist in Spain, Corsica, Pontus, Africa, the Eastern Archipelago, the West Indies, North and South America, we shall be inclined to admit that it arose from some secret spring in human nature, the effects of which may be modified by civilization, but are, perhaps, never entirely obliterated " (72, p. 281).

No comment is needed on this preposterous

"explanation", which ignores many of the recorded facts and grotesquely misinterprets the rest.

The proposed solution of the missionary Joseph Lafiteau (61) is no less fantastic, for he believed that the custom of couvade conserves a dim recollection of the doctrine of Original Sin. He adds some observations on the diffusion of the custom: "Ne pouvait-on pas présumer, d'une coûtume qui paraît si singulière, que de ces premiers peuples elle a passé à ces derniers [*i.e.* from the Old World to the New]; d'autant mieux que Strabon et la plupart des auteurs nous tracent le chemin que les Ibériens qui étaient venus d'Asie en Espagne anciennement nommée Ibérie, ont tenu pour retourner d'Espagne en Asie, où ce même nom d'Ibérie est resté au pays qu'ils occupèrent. N'ont-ils pas pu se transporter de là en Amérique?" (61, p. 49).

In 1889 couvade was connected with androgyny in a communication published by Tomlinson (121). Other correspondents added notes purporting to uphold this view, but in reality they have no bearing on couvade, and are merely cases of functional male mammary glands. It was apparently Tomlinson's suggestion that Keane had in mind, and which he seems to have taken seriously when he wrote: "A more recent view, based on the existence of the usually imperfect but sometimes functional mammary organs in the male, is that the progenitors of the mammalia were androgynous, and that the custom is a survival from the period when both sexes yielded milk and thus nourished their young" (53). Keane seems to have abandoned this view later, and vigorously maintains that the custom was independently evolved by all the peoples who practise it (54, p. 219).

The psychological explanations of the custom almost always fail to take into account all the data afforded by the diverse variations of the custom of couvade that have been noted earlier in this book. A generalization based on an ideal case that is a sort of mean between the extremes of form that the custom assumes cannot be applied as the explanation of the couvade in any particular locality. This facile method of disposing of a complex problem in a single paragraph is well illustrated by the following extract:

"Striking evidence of the effect of an association of ideas that is perfectly analogous to the one underlying the taboo of the mother-in-law is offered by a custom which is doubtless generally only local in scope and yet is found in the most diverse parts of the earth, thus showing plainly that it is autochthonous in character. I refer to the custom of so-called father-confinement, or 'couvade'. This custom prevails in various places, occurring even in Europe, where it is practised by the Basques of the Pyrenees, a remarkable fragment of a pre-Indo-Germanic population of Europe. Due, probably, to the heavier tasks which these people impose upon women, it here occasionally occurs in an exaggerated form. Even after the mother has already begun to attend to her household duties, the father, lying in the bed to which he has voluntarily retired, receives the congratulations of the relatives. Custom also demands that he subject himself to certain ascetic restrictions, namely, that he avoid the eating of certain kinds of food. The

custom of couvade is clearly the result of an idea-
tional association between husband and wife—one
that is absolutely analogous to that between the
two mothers of the married couple. The child owes
its existence to both father and mother. Both, therefore, must obey the regulations which surround
birth, and thus they are also subject to the same
taboo. Just as there is very commonly a taboo on
the mother and her new-born child, so also, in
regions where couvade exists, is this transferred
to the husband" (**139**).

The explanation put forward in the latter part
of this paragraph is an arbitrary generalization un-
supported by evidence, and the statements made,
moreover, are at variance with many of the recorded details of couvade.

Various other explanations have been put forward, usually based upon the form assumed by the
couvade custom in particular localities. Quandt,
for instance, imagined that the couvade arose out
of the desire of the women to have their men-folk
at hand at times of childbirth in order to help them
and to prevent them from going afield to hunt
large game, as the bringing in of the latter im-
posed much hard work upon the women. The men,
thus debarred from their usual pastimes and food,
found it better to take to their hammocks (**82**).
Firmin saw no more in the custom than the vanity
of men and the submissiveness of women (**36**)—the
exact contrary of Max Müller's view!—whilst
Marco Polo was told that it was only fair that the
husband should take a share in the pains and in-
conveniences of childbirth (**140**, p. **52**), and the
same explanation or justification is made in modern

times by the Sonjharas of the Central Provinces of India (96). These explanations involve the belief that the husband, by his lying-in, relieved his wife of pain, and made himself, it is not stated how, her scapegoat. Elsewhere magical means or witchcraft were directly applied by the nurse to transfer the pains of the mother to the father by means of the garments of the latter (71; 76). This transference of pain, or at least some relief to the mother, survived in a more innocent form, where the male garments effected their beneficent purpose without subjecting their owner to malignant witchcraft at the hands of a nurse (38, p. 251). The same idea is preserved in a belief in the north-east of Scotland " that the one who rose first on the morning after marriage carried all the pains and sorrows of child-bearing" (91).

Writing in 1896, Dr. Tautain rejected all the current explanations of the couvade, and put forward the opinion that the custom is really an adoption ceremony, whereby the father of the child claims his paternity (114). As we shall see, this view is not original, for long before Bachofen had hinted at it, and he used it to support his hypothesis, in which he was afterwards supported by Tylor, that the custom of couvade belongs to the turning-point of society when the matriarchal system was passing into the patriarchal, the father claiming his right by the fiction of making himself a second mother. In discussing the opinions of Bachofen and Tylor, we shall see that this "turning-point of society" is entirely theoretical, and fails to account for all the facts of the case. The simulation of birth as a form of adoption is certainly a most interesting custom, but it is difficult to see in it any genetic connection with couvade. Sir James Frazer has collected a number of instances of adoption rites.[1]

The theory, to which reference has been made, to account for couvade was put forward by Bachofen in 1861 and was generally accepted for many years, especially when Tylor, who had in the meantime proposed another which he then abandoned, gave it the weight of his support in a communication made to the British Association in 1888 (126; 127). Bachofen's theory may conveniently be summarized in Tylor's own words: "Looking at this position, I must now argue that the original interpretation of the couvade given by Bachofen in his great treatise in 1861, and supported by Giraud-Teulon, fits substantially with the facts, and is justified by them. He takes it to belong to the turning-point of society, when the tie of parentage, till then recognized in maternity, was extended to take in paternity, this being done by the fiction of representing the father as a second mother. He compares the couvade with the symbolic pretences of birth, which in the classical world were performed as rites of adoption. To his significant examples may be added the fact that among certain tribes the couvade is the legal form by which the father recognizes a child as his. Thus, this apparently absurd custom, which for twenty centuries has been the laughing-stock of mankind, proves to be not merely incidentally an indicator of the tendency of society from maternal to paternal, but the very sign and record of that vast change" (127, pp. 255-256).

[1] *Golden Bough*, 3rd ed. *The Magic Art*, vol. i. pp. 74 *sq.*

It may be explained that Tylor's return to
Bachofen's view was the result of an elaborate
method he devised of compiling schedules of the
systems of marriage and descent among some
350 peoples of the world. On this basis he applies
to his schedules a number of customs (of which
couvade is one), and, on the evidence of these
statistical results, he came to the conclusion that
the matriarchal system was older than the patriarchal, and that the custom of couvade marks, as
we have just seen, the transition of the one to the
other. Although this statistical method of inquiry
was received with acclamation at the time of its
first enunciation, it is not generally regarded as
sound at the present day. Other explanations that
are more in accordance with the evidence have
since been offered, but some later writers still
adhere to the Bachofen-Tylor theory (**29; 35; 43**).

Against this explanation, weighty considerations were brought forward by Roth (**94, p. 227**),
for cases of couvade are actually found amongst the
Arawaks and Melanesians, both of whom have
matrilineal descent, but another objection is well
expressed by Crawley in the following paragraph:
"Further, the custom would be too much of a legal
fiction if it meant all this originally; and early man
has not, as may easily be shown, any such lawyer-
like love of formality in matters of descent and
inheritance; like the animals, he attaches himself
to those with whom he happens to be born, and as
to inheritance, there is nothing to inherit. Doubtless, in certain cases, as amongst the Mundurucus,
the couvade may have come to be used as a method
whereby the father recognizes the child as his; but

this, besides being secondary, is not the same thing as a legal fiction asserting the father's rights as against the maternal system. It is rather a case of paternal pride. It would be expected that a people should themselves be aware of the fact, if assertion of paternal rights as against maternal were the object of the custom, the maternal system and counter-assertion being so obvious, but no tribe actually holds this meaning of the couvade" (24, pp. 181-182).

The explanation of Bachofen and Tylor was repeated in similar terms by Bastian, but he proposed a second alternative, namely, that the practice of couvade was an endeavour to cheat the demon of puerperal illness, and to protect the child against evil influences generally (9; 10; and cf. 185).

Another explanation was put forward by Tylor in 1865; and although he abandoned it in favour of Bachofen's theory in 1888, it has been found generally more acceptable, and has been followed by many writers of importance, notably by Sir James Frazer (38, vol. iv.), by the late Dr. E. S. Hartland (45), and by the late Mr. H. Ling Roth (94). Tylor suggested that the couvade custom expresses a physical bond between the father and his child, whereby, on the principle of sympathetic magic, any action of the father would react upon his offspring. This explanation certainly accounts for more features of the couvade than does the Bachofen theory, but it leaves untouched the many cases in which the father observes no restrictions before the birth of his child, and is merely pampered after the event. On the other hand, the terrible ordeal endured by the Caribs of the West Indies—

described by Rochefort (89), Du Tertré (115) and
Tylor (124; and see above, p. 93)—and the lesser
sufferings of the father elsewhere (*e.g.* the Land
Dyaks of Borneo, 99) cannot be explained on this
basis, for on the principle of sympathetic magic
the father's agonies would be endured by his child;
and it would be pushing the principle of sympathetic magic too far, and would make it altogether
too theoretical, to assume that, by the uncomplain-
ing endurance on the part of the father of scanty
and unsavoury diet, together with the physical pain
of scarification with its subsequent irritating dressing, the child would thereby acquire the power of
accomplishing such feats of endurance with forti-
tude!

Sir James Frazer holds that the term couvade
is applied to two entirely distinct series of customs,
although both are connected with childbirth. One
is the regimen observed by the father for the benefit
of the child to which he is closely related, and the
other is the simulation of childbirth by the father
in order to relieve the mother of the pains of labour.
He holds that both these customs are founded on
the principle of sympathetic magic; post-natal couvade is contagious magic and pre-natal is homoeo-
pathic or imitative. He rightly repeats that neither
custom has any bearing at all upon mother-right
or father-right (38, vol. iv. pp. 254-255.) Whilst
recognizing the dual nature of the couvade custom,
it seems to me that the two elements so often com-
bine, that for the purposes of examination they
must actually be taken as one. There certainly
seems to be much evidence in favour of Sir James
Frazer's explanation in interpreting the species of

couvade that merely takes the form of regimen and diet on the father's part, but can the same be said of the post-natal kind? Ploss has collected various instances of couvade, and classified them under two headings—those that are pleasant for the father, and those that are unpleasant (**78**, p. 207 ff.)—but this classification is quite artificial, and brings us no nearer to a real explanation. It is true that in the modified forms of couvade that survived till lately in France, Germany and Britain, the pains of the mother were believed to be transferred to the father by means of witchcraft or otherwise, but such an interpretation will hardly hold elsewhere. In the first place, the pains of childbirth amongst primitive peoples are not necessarily serious; the birth of a child to such a mother is not normally the prostrating and anxious crisis that befalls her civilized sisters. Innumerable instances could be quoted to prove that (provided the course of nature is normal and no pathological complications arise) the women of primitive peoples bear their children with a minimum of inconvenience and suffering, and, indeed, in many cases of recorded couvade it is expressly stated that the mother goes about her work as usual immediately after her delivery. In such circumstances, is there any need for the husband to lie-in for a considerable period, and to receive attentions that his wife neither requires nor expects, for the purpose of relieving her from sufferings that are not of a severe kind? Moreover, is there evidence of such a kindly sympathy between a man and his wife amongst primitive peoples? We find the couvade practised by the men of tribes who submit their kith and kin to ceremonies involving almost incredible physical pain, but there is no attempt to relieve the victims of their sufferings by sympathetic magic or otherwise. Why, then, should such tenderness be shown on an occasion that is, by comparison, almost painless? It is significant that the cases in which the transference of the pains of labour from the mother to the father is effected all occur in western European countries of advanced civilization, where childbirth is a far more serious affair than it is amongst primitive and uncivilized peoples.

Many of the observances performed by the husband of a pregnant woman seem rather destined to ensure the unimpeded delivery of the child than to relieve the mother of suffering. The untying of knots during a woman's pregnancy evidently is done in order to untie the child from hindrances to its proper entry into the world. In the Toumbuluh tribe of North Celebes, the husband, from the fifth month of his wife's pregnancy, is forbidden to tie fast knots or to sit with his legs crossed;[1] this is evidently a piece of sympathetic magic for the benefit of the quickening embryo. None of the many similar cases seems to refer to the wife, but rather to the child. If this is so, we cannot, it seems to me, maintain a sharp dividing line between customs based upon a sympathetic connection between father and child on the one hand, and those that are destined to relieve the mother of the dangers of childbirth on the other, that Sir James Frazer proposes.

[1] J. G. Frazer, *The Golden Bough*, 3rd ed. vol. iii. *Taboo and the Perils of the Soul*, p. 295. See the similar instances there collected, and below, p. 131, footnote 1.

We must now return to the other aspect of the explanation of the couvade custom, namely, the relationship of father to child. That there is a widespread belief in an intimate connection between father and child, both before and after the birth of the latter, is attested by many well-authenticated instances. In appraising the value of our evidence, however, we must be careful to distinguish between cases where the natives themselves have given this relationship between father and child as the reason for couvade, and these in which the explanation has merely been surmised, or even confidently stated, by modern writers. There is a tendency to regard all races as equals psychologically, and to explain all their actions, customs and beliefs by a single formula. The explanation put forward by Wundt (**139**; see above, p. 121) is an instance of this codification, and assumes that a widespread custom such as couvade can be interpreted in the same terms wherever it is found. Speaking of the couvade custom amongst the South American Indians, Dr. Karsten truly says: "An intricate sociological problem like the couvade cannot be solved with any single catch-word, be it this or that, and general summarizing explanations are of little use " (**52**, p. 465). It must be remembered that some of the explanations put forward are based upon the reasons assigned by the natives of various areas in which the custom is found. These must be used with the greatest caution. To quote Dr. Karsten again: "An Indian, when asked, for example, why he paints himself for certain occasions or practises tattooing, will in most cases give an evasive answer, or the explanation which he thinks looks most natural to the white man. . . . But we must be careful not to accept such vague answers to direct questions as real explanations " (52, p. 1).

This quotation refers to the South American Indians, but it applies with equal force to other parts of the world. A good instance of such an evasive explanation is that given by Marco Polo (140; above, p. 74). Here it was alleged that because the woman had gone through a period of hardship, it was only fair that the husband should do the same: actually, however, the man endured no suffering, but was pampered and congratulated.

I am far from denying that the belief in an intimate relationship between father and child may in many cases be the true explanation, or, at least, the most logical explanation, of the couvade; such instances as those related of the Abipones by Dobrizhoffer (31) and of the Nicobarese by Whitehead (134) leave no doubt on the matter.[1] But in other cases where modern writers have put forward this explanation, were they always really stating the local native belief, or were they merely generalizing from the accounts of others? It seems that many writers are too dogmatic in their assertions; they state as positive facts what may be, at best, no more than a probability. It is preferable to follow

[1] In this latter case, the principle of sympathetic magic is well expressed in the untying of knots, opening of boxes, etc. (see above, p. 129). This and similar practices are frequent amongst many peoples, the majority of whom are not known to practise the full couvade custom; in some cases they are performed by the husband, in others by both parents or by relatives. An interesting collection of instances has been made by Sir James Frazer, *The Golden Bough*, 3rd ed., *Taboo and the Perils of the Soul* (London, 1911), pp. 293 *et seq.*, and see below, p. 142.

the guidance of such writers as Sir Everard im Thurn, who has given us an excellent account of the couvade custom amongst the Guiana Indians (119). In presenting an explanation of the practice, he cautiously states this as his own belief, and does not say definitely that the interpretation he offers is really that of the natives themselves. His account is a model of what such a statement should be, and to the extract printed above (p. 95) I now add the concluding portion:

"No satisfactory explanation of its origin seems attainable. It appears based on a belief in the existence of a mysterious connection between the child and its father—far closer than that which exists between the child and its mother—and of such a nature that if the father infringes any of the rules of couvade for a time after the birth of a child, the latter suffers. For instance, if he eats the flesh of a water-haas (*Capybara*), a large rodent with very protruding teeth, the teeth of the child will grow like those of the animal; or if he eats the flesh of the spotted skinned labba, the child's skin will become spotted. Apparently there is also some idea that for the father to eat strong food, to wash, to smoke, or to handle weapons, would have the same result as if the new-born baby ate such food, washed, smoked, or played with edged tools " (119).

In this passage the author has summarized the observations of other writers, and tentatively offers them as a probable explanation. He does not dogmatize and state that these beliefs are actually held by the natives. In contrast with this passage, I will quote another, dealing with the same race, which, although mentioned with approval by Keane (54,

p. 368) seems to me to be a good instance of the confusion by modern writers between possibilities and certainties. A Guiana Indian, on the birth of a child, "calmly prepares for what he considers his duty. He must not hunt, shoot or fell trees for some time, because there is an invisible connection between himself and the babe, whose spirit accompanies him in all his wanderings, and might be shot, chopped, or otherwise injured unwittingly. He therefore retires to his hammock, sometimes holding the little one, and receives the congratulations of his friends, as well as the advice of the elder members of the community. If he has occasion to travel, he must not go very far, for the child spirit might get tired, and in passing a creek must first lay across it a little bridge or bend a leaf in the shape of a canoe for his companion. His wife looks after the cassava bread and pepper-pot, and assists others in reminding her husband of his duties. No matter that they have to go without meat for a few days, the child's spirit must be preserved from harm " (90).

On carefully examining all the instances of couvade assembled in the foregoing chapters, it will be evident that some of the proposed explanations are those of authors who had no direct native information, and merely generalized from previous writers' statements, or they are the result of direct questions put to the natives in which the answer practically was suggested by the query. It is quite clear that we cannot state that there is a uniform psychological belief innate in all primitive races in the existence of a mysterious relationship subsisting between father and child merely because we have evidence that in some cases this is, or may be, the case. Dr. Westermark considers that the custom of couvade implies this intimate relationship between father and child, and indicates plainly that those who practise it must be well aware of the principle that pregnancy is caused by sexual intercourse (133).[1] On the other hand, this does not explain why the husband's share in this union is magnified and that of his wife minimized, often to vanishing point. Some of the instances of modified pre-natal couvade that have been quoted seem to imply a close connection between husband and wife, rather than between father and child.

I take the view that the more elaborate forms of couvade in which the father simulates childbirth are not the development of the simpler forms that merely consist in restrictions in diet and occupation, but that the latter are degenerate survivals of the former.[2] In the oldest records of the custom that have survived, those of Strabo and of Diodorus, we have the couvade in its complete form, a form that in some localities has survived to the present day, whilst in others it has degenerated into mere segregation or food-restriction.

Crawley holds that the existing explanations of couvade err in not taking into account the woman's side of the question. He believes that couvade is merely one of the many expressions of the prin-

[1] It is worth noting that couvade does not appear to have been recorded amongst the various peoples who do not understand the function of the male element in procreation, as, for instance, various Australian tribes and some of the Melanesians, such as the inhabitants of the Trobriand Islands.

[2] Cf. W. H. R. Rivers, *History and Ethnology* (London, 1922), p. 5.

ciples of contact that underlie human relationships (24, pp. 182, 183). I cannot see, however, that his views bring us any nearer to an interpretation, and they seem to be merely another of those theoretical considerations that are held to be uniformally applicable to the human mind.[1]

We may, indeed, ask whether any of the attempted explanations hold good at the present day, and whether, in fact, the custom of couvade is susceptible of any explanation at all. There is a frequent tendency in man to rationalize his beliefs; he is ever attempting to explain away the often irrational actions that he habitually performs, and to convince himself and others that they have a rationalistic foundation. It seems to me that ethnologists make the false assumption that human beings are basically rational and logical, whereas the facts of everyday experience repeatedly belie such an idea. This point has been admirably summarized by Prof. Elliot Smith, whose words I will quote:

"It is a common fallacy to suppose that men's actions are inspired mainly by reason. The most elementary investigation of the psychology of everyday life is sufficient to reveal the truth that man is not, as a rule, the pre-eminently rational creature he is commonly supposed to be. He is impelled to most of his acts by his instincts, the circumstances of his personal experience, and the conventions of the society in which he has grown up. But once he has acted or decided upon a course of procedure he is ready with excuses in explanation and attempted justification of his motives. In most cases these

[1] As to Crawley's theories in general, see Mrs. B. Z. Seligman's remarks in *Man*, May 1928, No. 60 (pp. 87-88).

are not the real reasons, for few human beings attempt to analyse their motives or, in fact, are competent without help to understand their own feelings and the real significance of their actions. There is implanted in man the instinct to interpret for his own satisfaction his feelings and sensations, *i.e.* the meaning of his experience. But of necessity this is mostly of the nature of rationalizing, *i.e.* providing satisfying interpretations of thoughts and decisions, the real meaning of which is hidden."[1]

Human beings continue to enact irrational and obsolete customs and to perpetuate archaisms that are entirely bereft of their original significance. In England to-day numerous examples of such procedures could be quoted. We gravely enact strange and now meaningless rites on all sorts of ceremonial occasions: at the coronation of kings, at civic functions, at births, marriages and deaths, at the launching of ships, at the laying of foundation-stones and on scores of other occasions. Few people who perform and witness such ceremonies at the present day have the slightest knowledge even of their original, but now obsolete, significance. Assuming, therefore, that so strange a custom as couvade has been borrowed from one people by another in bygone ages, it is quite natural that its original meaning has been forgotten, and probable even that in many cases it has never been understood by those who adopted it. As Dr. Rivers truly says: "When customs are carried from their original home to other parts of the world, few of them sur-

[1] *The Evolution of the Dragon* (Manchester, 1919), p. 4. See also especially pp. 5-8.

vive unchanged, but suffer profound modification, some in the direction of progress, some in the direction of degeneration, and some in a direction that can hardly be described in terms either of progress or decay. . . . Many customs which were once supposed to be the products of a simple process of evolution among an isolated people have, in fact, behind them a long and tortuous history."[1]

The custom in the island of Cyprus mentioned by Plutarch affords a hint as to the possible ultimate origin of the couvade. In this case a man lies down, and by voice and gesture imitates a woman in travail, and it was clearly part of a religious ceremony.[2] In its transmission from place to place it was misunderstood and reinterpreted, whilst its original meaning was distorted or forgotten.[3] Parallel instances drawn from the transmission of other customs might be quoted;[4] and whilst I

[1] *History and Ethnology* (London, 1922), p. 5.

[2] In the Appendix to the second volume of *Adonis, Attis and Osiris* (*The Golden Bough*, 3rd ed. vol. vi. pp. 253-264), Sir James Frazer has collected a large and interesting series of examples of priests dressing and acting as women. There is no other case, however, of the curious procedure described by Plutarch. See also **24**, vol. i. pp. 250-252, 318-321.

[3] The same might apply with equal force to the Irish legend related in Chapter I.

[4] In mummification, for instance, many of the arbitrary technical details of the Egyptian method of embalming, details that in Egypt had a definite function, were slavishly followed in other countries where the modifications in method made these details serve no useful purpose whatever. I have called attention to such details in mummies from the Canary Islands (*Proc. Royal Soc. of Medicine*, vol. xx., 1927, pp. 851-854); from the Torres Straits Islands (*Annals of Archæology and Anthropology*, vol. xi., 1924, pp. 92-94); and from Australia and America (*Journ. Royal Anthrop. Inst.*, vol. lviii., 1928, pp. 115-138).

merely throw out the suggestion that couvade *may* originally have been part of a religious ceremonial which was afterwards invested with new and varied significance and made a mere family concern, I am conscious that this hint is very far short of an adequate explanation. In the meantime, until fresh facts come to enlighten us, we must, with Ploss (**78**, p. 211), humbly admit that the state of our knowledge regarding the original motive of the couvade custom is expressed by a single word— IGNORAMUS.[1]

[1] For some further remarks on the significance of couvade, see below, pp. 145–150.

## ADDENDA

SINCE the foregoing chapters have been set up in type, some further material relating to the custom of couvade has become available to me. The new matter supplements, but does not modify, the data presented in the text, and for the sake of completeness it will be convenient to deal with it as a series of addenda to the respective chapters.

CHAPTER I.—To the legends outlined in this chapter must be added another that is directly associated with the custom of couvade. The ancient tradition of the custom in the Iberian Peninsula does not rely solely upon the testimony of Strabo. There is an ancient legend attributed to the bard Lara (or Larus), who lived at the time of the Punic Wars when the Cantabri were the allies of Carthage. During the celebrations that followed the conclusion of peace between Rome and Carthage in 241, the bard is said to have sung the epic of Aitor, the traditional founder of the Basque race. The particular episode of the story that now concerns us may be summarized briefly as follows:

Aitor and his wife lived at the time when the great deluge overwhelmed the earth, and they took refuge from the rising waters on the summit of a high mountain, where they dwelt in impenetrable darkness amidst the clash of the elements. Here, in the cave that served as their home, a son was born, and as the tempest roared without, the infant's cries echoed through the cavern. Aitor's wife, fearing that prowling beasts, famished and daring, might enter the cave and snatch the child from her arms, would not suffer her husband to leave the cavern. Aitor accordingly took the infant, and, lying down with it upon his bed of skins, kept it warm on his ample breast. His wife, meantime, insisted on going herself in quest of food, feeling assured that the child would be safe in the arms of its strong protector. Thus said Aitor, "the sons of my race, out of respect for the hardships that befell their ancestor, have perpetuated as a commemorative custom that which foreign nations regard as so singular a usage, for they know not its origin. And thus, when a young mother leaves her bed of confinement, her husband at once takes her place with the new-born child, so that, by its inhaling the manly and paternal breath, the strength of the small and puny being is endowed with sympathetic influence." Such is the legendary origin of the Basque custom of couvade (**147**; cf. **179**, pp. **667-668**).

CHAPTER II.—Reference has been made (above, pp. 58 ff.) to the divergence of opinion upon the survival of couvade amongst the modern Basques. Many modern writers have denied the practice of couvade in the region of the Pyrenees, and to those who hold this opinion may be added Wentworth Webster, who dismisses the whole matter as a fable based upon the statement to Strabo (**183**). On the other hand, J. Augustin Chaho and Eugéne

Cordier, two writers who were intimately ac-
quainted with the customs of this region, have
definitely affirmed that the couvade was still practised in their time (**146; 150**).

Guest considered the practice of couvade in
antiquity by the Basques and by the Pontine
Tibareni as another point to be quoted in cor-
roboration of other evidence showing some connection between the two races (**157**).

With regard to Sardinia, although there is apparently no trace of couvade in a developed form,
there is, however, a custom that appears to be a
debased derivative of it. Von Maltzan has recorded
that when a Sardinian woman is confined, her husband eats his food from the same plate as his wife.
The woman being in bed, in order to share the
same dish, her husband must perforce go to bed
also (**169**).

Some further traces of the survival of the custom in Europe have been recorded by Letourneau.
"It is probable that more than one trace of this
'lying-in' still exists in Europe, in superstitious
and popular practices. Quite recently a Russian
has informed me that it is still in use in the Baltic
provinces, but naturally in a form of survival in
which the meaning is lost. It is, however, complete enough; the husband goes to bed, utters
groans and cries, and his neighbours hasten to his
side. And lastly, M. Léon Donnat told me lately
that he had discovered the couvade still practised
in the little island of Marken, in the Zuydersee"
(**163**, p. 318).

The avoidance by the husband of a pregnant
woman of handling edged tools and the untying of

knots are, as we have seen, practices closely related to, or associated with, couvade. It would therefore appear from the following extract from the narrative of an early eighteenth-century traveller that a dim recollection of the couvade existed at that time in Lapland: "To put a handle to an axe in the house of a lying-in woman was impious. The Laplanders cautiously provided against anything twisted or knotty in the garments of a person under such a situation, led by a vain imagination that such knots would render the birth of the woman more difficult" (162).

CHAPTER III.—The Rev. J. H. Weeks has recorded what he believes to be a survival of couvade amongst the Boloki of the Congo. After the birth of a child, the husband observes certain food prohibitions, and he is then said to be in a state of *liboi*, a noun derived from the verb *bwa*, "to be confined" (184).

A curious ceremony was witnessed in Madagascar by the seventeenth-century French traveller, François Cauche. An elaborate festival was held at a central spot, during which all the male children were brought from neighbouring districts to be circumcised. After the rite had been performed, the *fathers* of the infants returned in procession to their various villages, each carrying his child. The baby was tied by a cloth round the father's waist, and put its arms around the parent's neck. This method of carrying is that customary by the women. This is an instance of the father performing for his child what would normally be regarded as the mother's function, and it may possibly be a survival of the couvade tradition (145).

CHAPTER IV.—Reference was made to the practice of couvade by the aborigines of China, the Maiotzu (above, p. 74, and 32; 63). In this connection a Chinese drawing of the eighteenth century, now in the Victoria and Albert Museum, London, is of particular interest. It was published originally by Dr. S. W. Bushell (144), and by the kind permission of the director I reproduce it here (see Frontispiece). In the centre of the picture is a house, through the window of which may be seen a man lying on the bed nursing an infant, whilst his wife brings him refreshment on a tray. This picture is one of a series depicting the manners and customs of the Maiotzu.

A tradition of couvade amongst the Chinese proper has survived, but there is apparently no proof of its reality, confusion having arisen between the real Chinese and the Maiotzu. It is mentioned by Navarra (174), and more fully by Captain Neale, who refers to the "curious anecdote told of the Chinese, for the truth of which, however, no one has yet been able to vouch. They say when a Chinese lady is blessed with an increase in her family, from the moment of her accouchement the unhappy husband is put to bed also, and there detained for forty days, and during this delightful penance he is subjected to all the rigorous treatment of his better half. Should medicine be administered to her, he must partake of it also, and he is strictly confined to the same diet she is obliged to undergo" (73).

CHAPTER V.—Some interesting examples of present-day couvade amongst the Sea Dyaks of Borneo are given by the Rev. J. Perham (177), and amongst the Tuaran Dusans and the Endu Jakuns of the Malay Peninsula by Ivor Evans (155).

CHAPTER VI.—Some information regarding couvade amongst the Caribs of the West Indies, together with curious speculations as to the meaning of the custom, are given by the eighteenth-century traveller, T. de Chanvalon. He states, however, that he did not himself witness any instance of its observance (149). Some interesting modern testimony as to the couvade amongst the Caribs has been brought forward by Farabee (156). To the mention of couvade amongst the Jivaros of Ecuador may be added the following account by Orton: "An odd custom prevails among these wild Indians when an addition is made to the family circle. The woman goes into the woods alone, and on her return washes herself and the new-born babe in the river; then the husband immediately takes to his bed for eight days, during which time the wife serves him on the choicest dainties she can procure" (176).

Two actual cases of couvade, witnessed respectively by M. Mazé, Commissioner-General of French Guiana, in 1842 (on the River Oyapok), and by M. Voisin, Justice of the Peace, in 1852 (River Mana). In the latter case it is related that M. Voisin received hospitality for a night in the hut of a Galibi Indian. During the night, behind the partition of boughs that separated his hammock from the household of his host, a child was born. The mother uttered no sound, and at daybreak M. Voisin watched her go to the riverside with her infant. Here she first washed herself, then threw the child several times into the water, catching it as it rose to the surface and rubbing it with her hands. The husband meantime remained in his hammock, acting the invalid, and on his wife's return to the hut he received with the greatest seriousness all the attentions she lavished upon him (**172**, pp. 545-547).[1]

CHAPTER VII.—Reference was made on p. 108 to the story of a great flood: here it was stated that this legend originated in Mesopotamia. If the essential element in the story is held to be the destruction of mankind by a *deluge*, this statement is correct, because the Chaldean story is the oldest extant of this form of the legend.[2] If, on the other hand, the essential element in the legend is the destruction of rebellious men by an outraged deity (which may be accomplished in various ways: by slaughter, flood, fire, frost, etc.), then it is probable that the Egyptian story is the oldest in existence; and although the text that contains it dates only from the Nineteenth Dynasty, there is much reason for believing that it embodies an extremely ancient tradition.[3]

This point has no direct bearing upon couvade, but it is well to make it clear in view of the significance of the distribution of customs to which attention is called in this chapter.

CHAPTER VIII.—The views of many writers upon the significance of couvade have been dis-

---

[1] For some further instances of couvade in South America, see **148; 154; 160; 161; 175; 180.**

[2] For the sources of the story, see the preface to Dr. R. Campbell Thompson's *Epic of Gilgamish* (London, 1928).

[3] See the chapter "The Story of the Flood", by Prof. G. Elliot Smith, in his *Tutankhamen* (London, 1923), pp. 92-99, for a summary of this aspect of the legend.

cussed in this chapter, and for the sake of completeness the following additions may be made.

To the more fanciful interpretations of the custom detailed on pp. 118 ff. may be added that of Dr. Corre: "Cette bizarre comédie a sans doute pour but de faire oublier ses douleurs à la femme, de lui donner comme une innocente revanche de la réproduction" (151).

The view that was put forward long ago by Adolf Bastian (above, p. 126) that the practice of couvade was an endeavour to deceive malign spirits seems to have met with little support. In the numerous explanations of the custom that I have consulted, only one writer, Zmigrodzki, seems to have adopted it (185).

The great majority of writers, as we have seen, take a view similar to that of Bachofen and Tylor (above, p. 124) that couvade is in reality no more than an assertion of paternity, although they do not all go so far as to regard the custom as marking the transition from the matriarchal to the patriarchal régime. Maurel, for instance, after considering various theories, came to the conclusion that the true explanation of couvade must be the assertion of paternity (172). Ward, however, goes the whole length of the Bachofen-Tylor theory, and maintains that the custom marks the transition from mother- to father-right (182). Baron von Hellwald advanced the view that the mother and baby being connected by an obvious tie, the father made himself a second mother in order to assert his connection with the child, *i.e.* his paternity (158, p. 37). In a later work the same author explains couvade as having originally been a religious ceremony, a thanksgiving for delivery; but in course of time its original significance was forgotten, and it became merely a precaution taken by the parents for the welfare of the child (159, p. 362; and cf. the views of Lippert, 166; 167).

Dr. Kunike, whose paper on couvade has already been referred to (above, p. 113), makes the subject a peg on which to hang a long and discursive discussion, dealing more particularly with the custom as it is found in South America, but he makes no suggestion as to its origin or distribution in the Old World. He divides couvade into two types: the first, which he calls *imitatio naturae*, comprises the cases in which the husband goes to bed and feigns confinement; the second, involving only food-restrictions and other discipline, he regards as sympathetic magic for the benefit of the child (56, p. 556). In the long discussion that follows, couvade is mentioned in connection with the matriarchal and patriarchal systems, and with totemism, magic, etc., but the whole seems to me quite inconclusive. The term *imitatio naturae* seems an unfortunate one, for the husband's conduct in lying-up in his hammock is not an imitation of what actually occurs. Amongst many peoples of primitive culture the wife does not lie-in even for a short period: numerous instances have been quoted in this book in which the mother is delivered without trouble and without nursing or attention, often alone in the forest, and that after parturition she at once goes about her ordinary duties, bathes in the river, or otherwise actively occupies herself from the very moment of delivery. The couvade could only be called an *imitatio naturae* in the case of peoples of higher culture, where childbirth is a far more serious affair and involves the treatment of the mother, at least for several days, as an invalid (see above, p. 128).

Dr. Nathan Miller seems to me to have fallen into the same error when he says: "The variations of the actual conduct of the man are first of all an imitation of the mother's action. It is clear to the primitive man that to have a child it is necessary to be temporarily ill" (**173**, p. **25**). On the custom generally, he practically reverts to the Bachofen-Tylor view that "the couvade is merely one of the manifestations of that movement from the loosely organized matrilineal system that culminated finally in the patriarchal organization of the family and social life. It is a step in the evolution of the idea of 'paternity', later exfoliating into the extreme father-family of the nomadic culture-groups of antiquity. Yet it is objectionable to maintain that this is the 'very sign and record' [Tylor] of this momentous change in the history of culture. The couvade reflects a stage of development in which the paternal tie appears to have become an extremely intimate one. Von den Steinen, with Brazilian natives in mind, offers linguistic evidence to show that the 'child' means the 'little father', and this term is applied to the daughter as well. The child is thus a miniature, or part of the father" (**173**, pp. 24-25).

Chamberlain adopts the opinion of Von den Steinen that the child actually *is* the father, and concludes with a quotation from that author (**148**, p. 125). "The whole question of the 'couvade' and like practices finds its solution in these words of the author: 'The behaviour of the mother, according as she is regarded as more or less suffering, may differ much with the various tribes, while the conduct of the father is practically the same with all. She goes about her business, if she feels strong enough, suckles her child, etc. Between the father and child there is no mysterious correlation; the child is a multiplication of him; the father is duplicated, and in order that no harm may come to the helpless, irrational creature, a miniature of himself, he must demean himself as a child' " (111, p. 338).

This interpretation, founded on the linguistic indications of certain Brazilian tribes, even if it could be shown to explain the custom in that locality, will obviously not hold elsewhere. The point that most other writers have stressed is that so far from there being "no mysterious correlation" between father and child, there is indeed a close bond in which they see the basis of the custom and by which they explain it. Moreover, there are many instances of the couvade that prove that the man by lying-in simulates not his child, but his wife. It is not necessary now to call attention to the other points in which this explanation fails to cover the facts, nor to the objections to the paternity theory in general: these points have already been discussed (above, pp. 125 ff.). Nor is it necessary to comment upon the theory of Letourneau, who also accepts the affirmation of paternity as the explanation of couvade, and draws the curious inference that the custom "is, in short, a revolt of individualism against primitive communism" (163, p. 319); an inference that is all the stranger when his views on communism generally are taken into account.

Finally, I will quote the conclusions of a recent writer, Prof. B. Malinowski. So far as I am able to understand it, this paragraph seems to me to embody one of those highly theoretical hypotheses that soars far above the many and puzzling details of the custom itself and of its peculiar distribution. "Even the apparently absurd idea of *couvade* presents to us a deep meaning and a necessary function. It is of high biological value for the human family to consist of both father and mother; if the traditional customs and rules are there to establish a social situation of close moral proximity between father and child, if all such customs aim at drawing a man's attention to his offspring, then the couvade which makes man simulate the birth-pangs and illness of maternity is of great value and provides the necessary stimulus and expression for paternal tendencies. The *couvade* and all the customs of its type serve to accentuate the principle of legitimacy, the child's need of a father" (**168**).

# BIBLIOGRAPHY

1. *Academy, The,* vol. 42, London, 1892, pp. 389, 412, 437, 459, 542, 568.
2. *Academy, The,* vol. 25, London, 1884, p. 112.
3. ALBERUNI's INDIA, English ed. by E. S. Sachau, 2 vols., London, 1910, vol. i. p. 181 [Trübner's Oriental Series].
4. AMBROSETTI, JUAN, 'Los Indios Caingua del alto Paraná': *Boletin del Instituto Geografico Argentino,* t. xv., Buenos Aires, 1895, p. 32.
5. APOLLONIUS RHODIUS, 'Argonautica', bk. ii. lines 1010-1014, ed. R. Merkel, Leipsic, 1852, p. 75 [Teubner Series].
6. ARANZADI, T. DE, 'De la Covada en España', *Anthropos,* vol. v., Vienna, 1910, pp. 775-778.
7. BACHOFEN, J. J., 'Das Mutterrecht', Stuttgart, 1861, pp. 17, 225 [2nd ed., 1897].
8. BANCROFT, H. H., 'Native Races of the Pacific States of North America', 5 vols., London, 1875 ; vol. i. pp. 391, 412, 585.
9. BASTIAN, A., 'Zur vergleichenden Psychologie', *Zeitschrift für Völkerpsychologie und Sprachwissenschaft* [often quoted as 'Lazarus and Steinthal's Zeitschrift'], Bd. v., Berlin, 1868, pp. 153 ff.
10. BASTIAN, A., 'Matriarchat und Patriarchat', *Zeitschrift für Ethnologie,* Bd. viii., Berlin, 1886, pp. 331-341.
11. BATCHELOR, J., 'The Ainu of Japan', London, 1892, p. 44.
12. BEARDMORE, E., 'The Natives of Mouat, Daudai, British New Guinea', *Journal of the Anthropological Institute,* vol. xix., London, 1890, p. 462.
13. BERTHOLON, L., 'Les Formes de la famille chez les premiers habitants de l'Afrique du nord', Lyons, 1893.
14. BIET, A., 'Voyage de la France équinoxiale en l'isle de Cayenne', Paris, 1664, pp. 389-390.
151

152    WARREN R. DAWSON

15. BLACKMAN, W. S., 'Traces of Couvade in England', *Folk-Lore*, vol. xxix., London, 1918, pp. 319-320.

16. BLUMENTRITT, F., 'Sitten und Bräuche der Tagalen', Ausland, 1885, p. 1017.

17. BRETT, W. H., 'Indian Tribes of Guiana', London, 1868, pp. 101, 355.

18. BRIDGES, T., 'Manners and Customs of the Firelanders', London, 1866, p. 183.

19. BRISSAUD, J., 'La Couvade en Béarn et chez les Basques', *Revue des Pyrénées*, Toulouse, 1900, pp. 225-239.

20. CAIN, JOHN, *Indian Antiquary*, vol. iii., Bombay, 1874, p. 151.

21. CHAILLU, PAUL B. DU, 'Explorations and Adventures in Equatorial Africa', London, 1863, pp. 262, 305.

22. CHALMERS, JAMES, 'Pioneering in New Guinea', London, 1887, p. 165.

23. CODRINGTON, R. H., 'The Melanesians', Oxford, 1891, pp. 228-229.

24. CRAWLEY, A. E., 'The Mystic Rose', 2nd ed., revised and enlarged by T. Besterman, London, 1927, vol. ii. pp. 177-188.

25. CROOKE, W., 'Things Indian', London, 1906, pp. 59-60.

26. —— 'Natives of Northern India', London, 1907, p. 197.

27. DANCE, C. D., 'Chapters from a Guianese Log-book', Demerara, 1881, p. 249.

28. DARGUN, L. VON, 'Studien zum ältesten Familienrecht'. Erster Theil—'Mutterrecht und Vaterrecht', Leipsic, 1892, p. 18.

29. DENIKER, J., 'The Races of Man', London, 1900, p. 240.

30. DIODORUS SICULUS, 'Bibliotheca Historica', bk. v. ch. 14.

31. DOBRIZHOFFER, M., 'Historia de Abiponibus', Vienna, 1784, vol. ii. pp. 231 ff. [see above, p. 101, note 1].

32. DOUGLAS, R. K., 'Quaint Customs in Kweichow', *Cornhill Magazine*, vol. xxv., London, 1872, pp. 92-97.

33. DUNCAN, L. L., *Folk-Lore*, vol. x., London, 1889, p. 119.

34. EGEDE, HANS, 'A Description of Greenland, showing the Natural History, Situation, Boundaries and Face of the Country', London, 1745, p. 192.

35. ENCYCLOPÆDIA BRITANNICA, 11th ed., *art.* 'Couvade'.

# BIBLIOGRAPHY 153

**36.** Firmin, P., 'Description de Surinam', Amsterdam, 1769, vol. i. p. 81.

**37.** Fox, C. E., 'Social Organization in San Cristoval', *Journal of the Royal Anthropological Institute*, vol. xlix. (1919), p. 118.

**38.** Frazer, J. G., 'Totemism and Exogamy', London, 1910, vol. i. p. 73, vol. iv. pp. 244-255.

**39.** Giraud-Teulon, A., 'Les Origines du Mariage et de la Famille', Geneva and Paris, 1874, ch. iv. § 2, p. 193.

**40.** Gironière, P. de la, 'Twenty Years in the Philippine Islands', London, 1853, p. 73.

**41.** Haddon, A. C., 'A Batch of Irish Folk-lore', *Folk-Lore*, vol. iv., London, 1893, pp. 357-359.

**42.** —— and others, 'The Customs of the World', London, N.D., vol. ii. p. 1180.

**43.** Hambly, W. D., 'Origins of Education among Primitive Peoples', London, 1926, pp. 49, 75, 99, 125.

**44.** Hart, C. Van der, 'Reize rondom het eiland Celebes', 's Gravenhage, 1853, p. 137.

**45.** Hartland, E. S., 'The Legend of Perseus', 3 vols., London, 1894-96; vol. ii. 1895, pp. 400 ff.

**46.** Hodson, T. C., 'The Naga Tribes of Manipur', London, 1911, p. 177.

**47.** Hose, Charles, 'Natural Man: A Record from Borneo', London, 1926, p. 58.

**48.** Hutchinson, H. N., and others, 'The Living Races of Mankind', London, N.D. [1904], p. 564.

**49.** Hutton, J. H., 'The Sēma Nagas', London, 1921, p. 233.

**50.** Joest, W., 'Ethnographisches und Verwandtes aus Guyana', *Internationales Archiv für Ethnographie*, Bd. v., Suppt., Leiden, 1893, p. 98.

**51.** Jubanville, H. D'Arbois de, 'Les Guerriers d'Ulster en mal d'enfant ou la Neuvaine des Ulates', *Revue Celtique*, t. vii., Paris, 1886, pp. 225-230.

**52.** Karsten, Rafael, 'The Civilization of the South American Indians', London, 1926, ch. xiv. pp. 436-465.

**53.** Keane, A. H., *art.* 'Couvade', *Cassell's Encyclopædia*, vol. iii., London, N.D.

**54.** —— 'Ethnology', Cambridge, 1896, pp. 219, 368.

55. Koppers, W., 'Unter Feuerland Indianern', Stuttgart, 1924, p. 211.

56. Kunike, H., 'Das sogenannte Männerkindbett', *Zeitschrift für Ethnologie*, xliii., Berlin, 1911, pp. 546-563.

57. Labat, J. B., 'Nouveau Voyage aux isles de l'Amérique', The Hague, 1724, vol. ii. p. 123 [1st ed., Paris, 1713].

58. Laborde, A. L. J. de, 'Itinéraire descriptif de l'Espagne', 3rd ed., 6 vols., Paris, 1834, vol. i. p. 273.

59. —— 'View of Spain', 5 vols., London, 1809, vol. i. p. 383.

60. Laet, J. de, 'Novus Orbis seu descriptionis Indiae Occidentalis libri xviii.', Leiden, 1633, bk. xv. ch. xii. p. 544.

61. Lafiteau, J. F., 'Mœurs des sauvages américains', Paris, 1724, vol. i. p. 49.

62. Landtman, Gunnar, 'The Kiwai Papuans of British New Guinea', London, 1927, p. 224.

63. Lockhart, W., 'The Miautsze or Aborigines of China', *Transactions of the Ethnological Society*, N.S. vol. i., London, 1861, p. 181.

64. Lubbock, John [later Lord Avebury], 'Origin of Civilisation and the Primitive Condition of Man', London, 1870, pp. 10 *sq.*

65. —— 'On the Social and Religious Condition of the Lower Races of Man', *British Association, Liverpool Meeting, 1870*, pp. 6-7 of the reprint.

66. Man, E. H., 'The Nicobar Islanders', *Journal of the Anthropological Institute*, vol. xviii., London, 1889, p. 368.

67. —— 'The Aboriginal Inhabitants of the Andaman Islands', *Journal of the Royal Anthropological Institute*, vol. xii., London, 1882, p. 87.

68. Martius, C. F. P. von, 'Beiträge zur Ethnographie und Sprachenkunde Amerikas zumal Brasiliens', 2 vols., Leipsic, 1867.

69. Michel, Francisque, 'Le Pays basque, sa population, sa langue, ses mœurs, sa littérature et sa musique', Paris, 1857, p. 201.

70. Modigliani, E., 'Viaggio di Elio Modigliani pubblicato a cura della Società Geografica Italiana', Rome, 1892, p. 555.

71. Mooney, James, 'The Medical Mythology of Ireland', *Proceedings of the American Philosophical Society*, vol. xxiv. p. 146.

72. MÜLLER, F. MAX, 'Chips from a German Workshop', vol. ii., London, 1867, pp. 274 *sq.*

73. NEALE, F. A., 'Narrative of a Residence at the Capital of the Kingdom of Siam', London, 1852, p. 155.

74. NORDENSKIÖLD, E., 'Indianer och hvita i nordostra Bolivia', Stockholm, 1911, p. 167.

75. PARKINSON, R., 'Dreissig Jahre in der Südsee', Stuttgart, 1907, p. 189.

76. PENNANT, THOS., 'A Tour of Scotland and a Voyage to the Hebrides in 1772', London, 1774, p. 79.

77. PERELAER, M. T. H., 'Ethnographische beschrijving der Dajaks', Zalt-Bommel, 1870, p. 38.

78. PLOSS, H., 'Das Kind in Brauch und Sitte der Völker', 3rd ed., revised by B. Renz, Leipsic, 1911, vol. i. pp. 191-211.

79. —— and BARTELS, M., 'Das Weib in der Natur- und Völkerkunde', Berlin, 1927, vol. i. pp. 510, 706, 756; ii. 473, 482; iii. 58.

80. PLUTARCH, 'Theseus', cap. xx., *Plutarchii Vitae Parallelae*, ed. C. Sintenis, vol. i., Leipsic, 1884, p. 17 [Teubner Series].

81. POWELL, WILFRED, 'Wanderings in a Savage Country: or, Three Years amongst the Cannibals of New Britain', London, 1884, p. 207.

82. QUANDT, CHRISTLIEB, 'Nachricht von Surinam und seinen Einwohnern sonderlich den Arawaken und Karaiben', Gorlitz and Leipsic, 1808, pp. 252-253.

83. QUATREFAGES, A. DE, 'Souvenirs d'un naturaliste', *Revue des Deux Mondes*, t. v., Paris, 1850, p. 1084.

84. REINACH, SALOMON, 'L'Amphidromie', *L'Anthropologie*, t. x., Paris, 1899, pp. 663-670.

85. RHYS, JOHN, 'The Hibbert Lectures, 1886', 2nd ed., London, 1892, pp. 140, 363, 627-629, 678.

86. RIPLEY, A. Z., 'The Races of Europe', London, 1900, p. 182.

87. RIVERO, JUAN, 'Historia de las misiones de los llamos de Casanare y los rios Orinoco y Meta', Bogota, 1883, p. 347.

88. RIVERS, W. H. R., 'History of Melanesian Society', Cambridge, 1924, vol. i. p. 146.

**89.** Rochefort, C. de, 'Histoire naturelle et morale des isles Antilles de l'Amérique', by L. de Poincy: 2nd ed. revised by C. de R., Rotterdam, 1665, p. 550 [3rd ed., 1681].

**90.** Rodway, J., 'In the Guiana Forest', London, 1895, pp. 25-26.

**91.** Rorie, David, 'Scottish Folk Medicine', § iv., *Caledonian Medical Journal*, vol. xiii., Glasgow, 1926, p. 91.

**92.** Roscoe, J., 'The Bagasu and other Tribes of the Uganda Protectorate', Cambridge, 1924, p. 24.

**93.** Rose, H. J., 'Couvade in Ontario', *Folk-Lore*, vol. xxix., London, 1918, p. 87.

**94.** Roth, H. Ling, 'On the Signification of Couvade', *Journal of the Anthropological Institute*, vol. xxii., London, 1893, pp. 204-243.

**95.** Roth, Walter E., 'An Enquiry into the Animism and Folklore of the Guiana Indians', *American Bureau of Ethnology*, *30th Annual Report*, Washington, 1915, p. 321.

**96.** Russell, R. V., 'Tribes and Castes of the Central Provinces of India', London, 1916, vol. iv. p. 511.

**97.** St. Cricq, De, 'Voyage de Pérou au Brésil par les fleuves Ucayali et Amazone, Indiens Conibos', *Bulletin de la Société Géographique*, 4th ser. vol. vi., Paris, 1853, p. 288.

**98.** St. John, Spencer, 'Life in the Forests of the Far East', 2 vols., 2nd ed., London, 1862, vol. i. p. 170.

**99.** —— 'Wild Tribes of the North-West Coast of Borneo', *Transactions of the Ethnological Society*, N.S. vol. ii., London, 1863, p. 233.

**100.** Schadenberg, A., 'Beiträge zur Kentniss der im Innern Nordluzons lebenden Stämme', *Verhandlungen der Berliner Gesellschaft für Anthropologie*, 1888, p. 35.

**101.** Schomburgk, Richard, 'Reisen in Britisch Guiana in dem Jahren 1840-1844', 3 vols., Leipsic, 1847-48, vol. ii.

**102.** Schreiber, A., 'Die Insel Nias', *Dr. A. Petermann's Mittheilungen aus Justus Perthes' Geographischer Anstalt*, Bd. xxiv., Gotha, 1878, p. 50.

**103.** Seligman, C. G., 'The Melanesians of British New Guinea', Cambridge, 1910, p. 86.

**104.** Simson, A., 'Notes on the Piojes of the Putumayo', *Journal of the Anthropological Institute*, vol. viii., London, 1879, p. 222.

105. SIMSON, A., 'Notes on the Jivaros and Canelos Indians', *Ibid.* vol. ix., 1880, p. 388.

106. SKEAT, W. W., 'Malay Magic', London, 1900, p. 345.

107. SOUTHEY, R., 'History of Brazil', 3 vols., London, 1810-19, vol. i. p. 238.

108. SMITH, G. ELLIOT, 'The Migrations of Early Culture', Manchester, 1915, pp. 129-130.

109. SPIX, J. B., and MARTIUS, C. F. P. VON, 'Reise in Brasilien, 1817-1820 ' (3 vols., with continuous pagination), Munich, 1823-31.

110. ——— 'Travels in Brazil', translated by H. E. Lloyd, 2 vols., London, 1824, vol. ii. p. 247.

111. STEINEN, KARL VON DEN, 'Unter den Naturvölkern Zentral-Brasiliens: Reisenschilderung und Ergebnisse der zweiten Schingú-Expedition, 1887-88', Berlin, 1894, pp. 334, 338-434, 503.

112. STELLER, G. W. 'Beschreibung an der Lande Kamtschatka', Frankfort, 1774, p. 351.

113. STRABO, 'Geographica', Bk. iii. cap. iv. § 17.

114. TAUTAIN, DR., 'La Couvade', *L'Anthropologie*, t. vii., Paris, 1896, pp. 118-119.

115. TERTRÉ, J. B. DU, 'Histoire générale des Antilles', 4 vols., Paris, 1667-71, vol. ii. p. 371.

116. THEVET, ANDRÉ, 'Cosmographie universelle', 2 vols., Paris, 1575, pp. 915-916.

117. THIERS, J. B., 'Traité des superstitions', Paris, 1679, p. 327.

118. THOUAR, A., 'Auf der Suche nach den Resten der Crevaux'schen Expedition', *Globus*, Bd. xlviii., Brunswick, 1885, p. 35.

119. THURN, EVERARD IM, 'Among the Indians of Guiana', London, 1883, pp. 217-219.

120. THURSTON, EDGAR, 'Ethnographic Notes in Southern India', Madras, 1906, pp. 547-551.

121. TOMLINSON, C., *Notes and Queries*, 7th series, vol. viii., London, 1889, p. 442 [cf. *Ibid.* vol. ix. pp. 9-10, 54-55].

122. TORDAY, E., 'On the Trail of the Bushongo', London, 1925, p. 173.

123. TSCHUDI, J. J. VON, 'Peru: Reiseskizzen aus den Jahren 1838-1842', St. Gall, 1846, vol. ii. p. 235.

158     WARREN R. DAWSON

**124.** TYLOR, E. B., 'Researches into the Early History of Mankind', London, 1865, pp. 287-297.

**125.** —— 'Primitive Culture', 2nd ed. London, 1873, vol. i. p. 84.

**126.** —— 'On a Method of Investigating the Development of Institutions applied to Laws of Marriage and Descent', *Report, British Association, Bath, 1888*, London, 1889 (Sect. H, 'Anthropology').

**127.** —— The same paper as **126**, with diagrams, *Journal of the Anthropological Institute*, vol. xviii., London, 1889, pp. 254-256.

**128.** VALERIUS FLACCUS, 'Argonautica', bk. v. lines 147-149, ed. Otto Kramer, Leipsic, 1913, p. 112 [Teubner Series].

**129.** VENEGAS, MIGUEL, 'A Natural and Civil History of California, translated out of the Original Spanish', London, 1759, pp. 81-82.

**130.** VINSON, JULIEN, 'La Couvade de chez les Basques', in Hovelacque and Vinson, *Études de linguistique et d'ethnographie*, Paris, 1878.

**131.** WADDELL, L. A., 'The Tribes of the Brahamaputra Valley', *Journal of the Asiatic Society of Bengal*, vol. lxix., Calcutta, 1901, p. 3.

**132.** WAITZ, THEODOR, 'Introduction to Anthropology', ed. by Frederick Collingwood, London, 1863, vol. i. pp. 257-258.

**133.** WESTERMARK, E., 'History of Human Marriage', 3 vols., London, 1921, vol. i. p. 287.

**134.** WHITEHEAD, G., 'In the Nicobar Islands', London, 1924, pp. 115 *sq.*

**135.** WILKEN, G. A., 'De Couvade bij de Volken den Indisch-Archipel', *Bijdragen voor de Taal, Land, en Volkerkunde*, Batavia, 1889, ser. 5, vol. iv. pp. 250-266.

**136.** WILLIAMS, M. MONIER, 'Religious Life and Thought in India', London, 1883, p. 229.

**137.** WINDISCH, E., *Berichte der K. Säch. Gesellschaft der Wissenschaften (Phil.-Hist. Classe)*, 1884, pp. 336 ff.

**138.** WOLF, J. W., 'Beiträge zur deutschen Mythologie', Bd. i., Leipsic, 1852, p. 251.

**139.** WUNDT, W., 'Elements of Folk Psychology', translated by E. L. Schaub, London, 1916, p. 198.

**140.** YULE, HENRY, 'The Book of Ser Marco Polo the Venetian', London, 1871, vol. ii. pp. 52, 57.

**141.** ZAMACOLA, D. J. A. DE, 'Historia de les nacions Bascas', 3 vols., Auch, 1818, vol. iii. p. 46.

**142.** ZUCCHELLI, A., 'Relazione de viaggio e missione di Congo', Venice, 1712, 7th rel. § xv. p. 118.

**143.** —— 'Merckwürdige Missions- und Reise-beschreibung nach Congo', Frankfort, 1715, pp. 165-166.

## ADDENDA

**144.** BUSHELL, S. W., 'Chinese Art', vol. ii., London, 1906, p. 145 and Fig. 134.

**145.** CAUCHE, F., 'Relation du voyage que François Cauche a fait à Madagascar, isles adjacentes et coste d'Afrique, recueilly par le Sieur Morisot', in the volume entitled *Relations véritables et curieuses*, Paris, 1651, pp. 51 ff.

**146.** CHAHO, J. AUGUSTIN, 'Voyage à Navarre pendant l'insurrection des Basques', Paris 1836, p. 309.

**147.** —— 'Histoire primitive des Euskariens-Basques', Bayonne, 1847, t. i. pp. 173 ff., especially pp. 191, 192.

**148.** CHAMBERLAIN, A. F., 'The Child and Childhood in Folk Thought', New York, 1896, p. 124.

**149.** CHANVALON, T. de, 'Voyage à la Martinique . . . fait en 1751', etc., Paris, 1763, p. 52.

**150.** CORDIER, E., 'Le Droit de la famille aux Pyrénées', *Revue historique de droit français et étranger*', t. v., Paris, 1859, p. 370.

**151.** CORRE, A., 'La Mère et l'enfant dans les races humaines', Paris, 1882, p. 91.

**152.** CRANZ, D., 'Histoire von Grönland', Berlin, 1765, p. 275 [Eng. ed., 'History of Greenland', London, 1767].

**153.** DALTON, E. T., 'Descriptive Ethnology of Bengal', Calcutta, 1872, p. 190.

**154.** ERNST, A., 'Über die ethnographische Stellung der Guajaro-Indianer', *Zeitschrift für Ethnologie*, Bd. xix., Berlin, 1887, p. 442.

**155.** EVANS, IVOR H. N., 'Studies in Religion, Folk-lore and Custom in British North Borneo and the Malay Peninsula', Cambridge, 1923, pp. 13, 268.

**156.** FARABEE, W. CURTIS, 'The Central Caribs', Philadelphia, 1924, pp. 78-80 [*University of Pennsylvania, Anthropological Publications*, vol. x.].

**157.** GUEST, EDWIN, 'Origines Celticae', 2 vols., London, 1883, vol. i. p. 63.

**158.** HELLWALD, BARON F. VON, 'Culturgeschichte in ihrer natürlichen Entwicklung bis zur Gegenwart', Ausburg, 1875, pp. 36, 37.

**159.** —— 'Die menschliche Familie', Leipsic, 1889, p. 362.

**160.** KOCH-GRÜNBERG, THEODOR, 'Die Anthropophagie der Südamerikanischen Indianer', *Internationales Archiv für Ethnographie*, Bd. xii., Leiden, 1899, pp. 79-82

**161.** —— 'Vom Roroima zum Orinoco', 4 Bde., Bd. iii., Stuttgart, 1923, pp. 135-138, 363.

**162.** LEEM, C. [LEEMIUS], 'Account of Danish Lapland', in John Pinkerton, *General Collection of Voyages and Travels*, vol. i., London, 1808, p. 483.

**163.** LETOURNEAU, CHARLES, 'The Evolution of Marriage and of the Family', London, 1891, pp. 316-319 [*Contemporary Science Series*; translation of 'L'Évolution du mariage et de la famille', Paris, 1888 (pp. 394 ff.)].

**164.** —— 'Sociology based upon Ethnography', London, 1893, pp. 385, 386, 387, 396.

**165.** —— 'La Femme à travers les âges', *Revue de l'École d'Anthropologie de Paris*, t. ix., Paris, 1901, pp. 273-290.

**166.** LIPPERT, JULIUS, 'Die Geschichte der Familie', Stuttgart, 1884, p. 17.

**167.** —— 'Kulturgeschichte der Menschheit', 2 Bde., Stuttgart, 1887, Bd. ii. pp. 312, 313.

**168.** MALINOWSKI, B., 'Sex and Repression in Primitive Society', London, 1927, pp. 215-216.

**169.** MALTZAN, H. F. VON, 'Reise auf der Insel Sardinien', Leipsic, 1869, p. 56.

**170.** MASON, OTIS T., 'Woman's Share in Primitive Culture', New York, 1894, p. 205.

171. MATEER, S., 'The Pariah Caste in Travancore', *Journal of the Royal Asiatic Society*, new ser. vol. xvi., London, 1884, p. 188.

172. MAUREL, DR., 'De la couvade', *Bulletins de la Société d'Anthropologie de Paris*, 3rd ser. t. vii., Paris, 1884, pp. 542-550.

173. MILLER, NATHAN, 'The Child in Primitive Society', London, 1928, pp. 23-25.

174. NAVARRA, B., 'China und die Chinesen', Bremen, 1901, p. 996.

175. ORBIGNY, A. D', 'L'Homme américain', Paris, 1839, t. i. p. 237.

176. ORTON, J., 'The Andes and the Amazon: or, Across the Continent of South America', New York, 1870, p. 172.

177. PERHAM, JOHN, 'Seventeen Years among the Sea Dyaks of Borneo', London, 1911, pp. 96 ff.

178. ROUGEMONT, F. DE, 'Le Peuple primitif', 3 vols., Geneva, 1855, t. ii. p. 420.

179. ROYER, CLÉMENCE, and others, 'Discussion sur la couvade', *Bulletins de la Société d'Anthropologie de Paris*, 3rd series, t. v., Paris, 1882, pp. 636 ff, 662 ff.

180. SCHMIDT, MAX, 'Indianerstudien in Central-Brasilien', Berlin, 1905, p. 438.

181. THOMAS, J. W., 'Sitten und Aberglauben auf Nias', *Globus*, Bd. xl., Brunswick, 1881, p. 13.

182. WARD, LESTER F., 'Pure Sociology', New York, 1903, pp. 200, 213, 343-344.

183. WEBSTER, WENTWORTH, 'Basque Legends', London, 1877, p. 232.

184. WEEKS, JOHN H., 'Among Congo Cannibals', London, 1913, p. 132.

185. ZMIGRODZKI, M. VON, 'Die Mutter bei den Völkern des arischen Stammes', Munich, 1886, p. 267.

# APPENDIX

PRINTED below are translations of the French passages and fresh translations of the Greek and Latin.

FRENCH, pp. 50–51.—". . . among the Cyprians, a man takes to his bed and imitates the cries and contortions of a woman in labor."

GREEK, footnote, p. 51.—"Theseus came back and, very grief-stricken, left money for the islanders, and ordered them to make a sacrifice to Ariadne and to set up two little human images, one silver and the other bronze. He also ordered that during the second sacred ceremony of the month Gorpiaeus, one of the young men should lie down and make the kind of sounds and do the kind of things a woman in labor does."

GREEK, footnote, p. 54.—"The Scythians who plundered the temple at Ascalon, and their descendants forever to this day, were afflicted by the god with female disease. The Scythians themselves say that this is why they are sick, and those who travel to the Scythian region see among them how it happens that the Scythians call them Enarees [womanlike men, or androgynes]."

GREEK, footnote, p. 57.—"But most incredible is what goes on among them concerning the birth of children. When the woman gives birth, no attention at all is given to her about the delivery; but her husband falls down as though he were ill and giving

163

birth for a set number of days, as though his own body were in terrible pain."

FRENCH, p. 58.—Laborde says "the Cantabrian women carry the heaviest loads; they cultivate the champagne, work the fields, and do not neglect any sort of chore; they get up immediately after giving birth and wait on their husbands who take to their beds in their wives' place. This custom which was also common among the natives of Navarre is impossible to fathom."

GREEK, footnote, p. 58.—"These things are common to the Celtic and Thracian and Scythian races, and common too is what courage or endurance means both for men and women. The women do the farming, and when they are giving birth, they take care of the men, and the men lie down in bed instead of them."

FRENCH, p. 60.—"'au lit et en couche'": "'in bed and in labor'"

FRENCH, p. 60.—"*faire la couvade*": "doing the hatching"

FRENCH, p. 60.—"Il se met au lit quand sa femme est en couche": "He takes to his bed when his wife is in labor."

FRENCH, pp. 60–61.—"When a woman is in labor, her husband's breeches are placed on her so that she can deliver painlessly."

GREEK, footnote 1, p. 67.—"Straightway they rounded the headland of Genetaean Zeus and made it safely past the land of the Tibareni. There, when women bear children by their husbands, the men fall into bed in agony, binding up their heads, while their wives take care of them with food and even draw the bath for childbirth."

LATIN, footnote 2, p. 67.—"From there they passed the headland of Genetaean Jupiter, and thence the green lakes of the land of the Tibareni, where a pregnant woman binds up her husband's head with a useless headband and takes care of him when the delivery is over."

FRENCH, p. 98.—"When the Petivarian women are in labor, their husbands go to bed and are greeted courteously by all their neighbors and are cared for as fully and tenderly as if they were women."

LATIN, book title, footnote, p. 101.—*The History of the Abipones, a warlike equestrian nation in Paraguay—a history chock-full of copious observations on the barbarian tribes, cities, rivers, wild beasts, amphibians, insects, extraordinary snakes, fish, birds, trees, plants, and other peculiar features of this same province.*

FRENCH, p. 120.—"Couldn't one presume, from such a peculiar custom, that it was brought from the Old World to the New; all the better that Strabo and the majority of authors trace for us the route the Iberians who came from Asia to Spain, formerly known as Iberia, took to return from Spain to Asia, where this same name, Iberia, remained in the land they occupied. Couldn't they have transported themselves from that place to America?"

FRENCH, p. 146.—"This bizarre enactment is surely designed to let the woman forget her pain, to give her a sort of innocent revenge on reproduction."

# INDEX

# FOR RELATED READING

## THOSE WOMEN
### Nor Hall

This book is about the God who electrifies women. And the Dionysian charge that surfaces in the lives and writing of Jungian analyst Linda Fierz-David, classicist Jane Ellen Harrison, poet H.D.—women who are related by affinity to those women who embraced Jung's depth psychology with their whole lives. Hall here uses the ten scenes of dramatic initiation in a Pompeiian mystery chamber to frame the experiences of death, maenadic madness, and change that occur to women in the midlife constellation of Dionysos, the Loosener. Color plates. (84 pp.)

## DIONYSUS: MYTH AND CULT
### Walter F. Otto

An examination of Dionysiac worship in the maenad cults, the mask, tragedy and theatre, in silence, pandaemonium and somber madness, through the vine and juices of vegetative nature, and in relation with woman, especially Ariadne. A full, authoritative phenomenology of the God by a rare scholar whose understanding carries the reader into participation. Plates, notes, index. (xxi, 243 pp.)

## PUER PAPERS
### James Hillman, ed.

The *puer aeternus*, the radiant youth, aloof, sensitive, and eternal: an archetype in myth and poetry, a symptom in psychotherapy, a figure in dreams, a theme in biography. In this collection of nine papers, analyst, mythologist, literary critic, and psychotherapist examine the full range of puer phenomena. A practical book relevant to diagnosis, dream analysis, hermeneutics, societal movements, and literary criticism (e.g., puer figures in Melville and Joyce). Includes Hillman's "Senex and Puer," "Peaks and Vales," "Puer Wounds and Ulysses' Scar," and "Notes on Opportunism," Tom Moore on Artemis's puer, as well as "American Icarus" by the famous Harvard psychologist Henry Murray. Indexed. (246 pp.)

Spring Publications, Inc. • P. O. Box 222069
Dallas, TX 75222